Essentials of Social Work Policy Practice

Essentials of Social Work Practice Series

Essentials of Child Welfare
Rodney A. Ellis, Catherine N. Dulmus, and John S. Wodarski

Essentials

of Social Work

Policy Practice

Cynthia J. Rocha

 John Wiley & Sons, Inc.

Published by John Wiley & Sons, Inc., Hoboken, New Jersey.
Published simultaneously in Canada.

Wiley Bicentennial Logo: Richard J. Pacifico

For general information on our other products and services please contact our Customer Care Department within the United States at (800) 762-2974, outside the United States at (317) 572-3993 or fax (317) 572-4002.

Wiley also publishes its books in a variety of electronic formats. Some content that appears in print may not be available in electronic books. For more information about Wiley products, visit our web site at www.wiley.com.

Library of Congress Cataloging-in-Publication Data

Rocha, Cynthia J.
    Essentials of social work policy practice / by Cynthia J. Rocha.
        p. cm. — (Essentials of social work practice series)
    ISBN-13: 978-0-471-75220-2 (pbk.)
    1. Social work education. 2. Social case work—Management. 3. Social services—Political aspects. 4. Social policy. I. Title.
    HV11.R52 2007
    361.3 2—dc22
                                                                                                2006037550

Printed in the United States of America.

10   9   8   7   6   5   4   3   2   1

To my students, who have taught me so much.
To adapt a phrase from Gandhi,
"There go my students and I must follow them,
for I am their teacher."

CONTENTS

SERIES PREFACE

I n the *Essentials of Social Work Practice* series, our goal is to provide readers with books that will deliver key practical information in an efficient,
accessible style. The series features books on a variety of topics of
interest to clinical social workers, such as child welfare, case management,
social work policy and practice, to name just a few. For the experienced
professional, books in the series offer a concise yet thorough overview
of a specific area of expertise, including numerous tips for best practices.
Students will find here a prioritized assembly of all the information and
techniques that must be at one's fingertips to practice knowledgeably, efficiently, and ethically in the social work field.

Wherever feasible, visual cues highlighting key points are utilized along-
side systematic, step-by-step guidelines. Chapters are focused and succinct.
Topics are organized for an easy understanding of the essential material
related to a particular practice area. Theory and research are continually
woven into the fabric of each book, but always to enhance the practical application of the material, rather than sidetrack or overwhelm readers. With
this series, we aim to challenge and assist readers engaged in providing
social work services to aspire to the highest level of proficiency by arming
them with the tools they need for effective practice.

The Essentials of Social Work Policy Practice is a skill-based book written for
students in policy practice classes and is an easy reference guide for social work
practitioners. The book provides basic principles of policy practice, a planning
process on how to plan for and implement specific change strategies, and the
skills to work in a variety of policy settings. Chapters 3 through 6 provide step-

by-step instructions on skills that can be used across organizations and policy levels. Chapters 7 through 10 provide specific strategies for working with the community, in organizations, and at the legislative, bureaucratic, and judicial levels of government. Case examples are provided throughout to give readers ideas on how to use the techniques discussed.

ACKNOWLEDGMENTS

I want to acknowledge the great support of my husband, Bill, and my daughter, Clarissa. Former county commissioner Madeline Rogero, Executive Director of NASW-TN chapter Karen Franklin, and law professor Fran Ansley read selected chapters and gave excellent suggestions. Finally, I want to acknowledge Natalie Crippen, who is the best administrative assistant ever! Lots of other people have contributed to the ideas in this book, more than I can name here—but you will find many of their stories within.

Essentials of Social Work Policy Practice

One

RATIONALE AND DESCRIPTION OF POLICY PRACTICE

Although there is not complete agreement on what constitutes policy practice, there is general agreement that social workers must assume policy roles and learn to perceive policy practice as among the skills of a practicing social worker, not the purview of a policy expert. Bruce Jansson first developed the concept of policy practice for social workers in the mid-1980s as a specific intervention designed to make changes in the political arena (Jansson, 2003). Wyers (1991) and Figueira-McDonough (1993) began calling for an increased recognition of policy practice interventions as a necessary continuum of skills for social workers to help clients at larger systems levels. There is now a clearer understanding that social workers may be called on to utilize policy practice skills, regardless of their specialized areas of interest. For the purpose of this book, policy practice is defined as a change approach that uses advocacy and community practice techniques to change programs and policies at multiple systems levels, targeting communities, local, state, and federal governments, agencies, bureaucracies, and the courts.

Conceptualizing Policy Practice

There are many ways that authors have conceptualized the various components of policy practice; as political social work, class advocacy, political advocacy, community practice, social action, and legislative advocacy, to name a few. In 1991, Wyers attempted to integrate some of the micro- and macro-approaches to policy practice by defining a model that included a continuum of policy practice skills, including (a) a policy expert—one who conducts policy analysis and provides expert knowledge and skills pertaining to the policy arena, (b) the social worker as a change agent working in an external environment, meaning that she or he works outside of her or his organization advocating for legislative initiatives, working in policy development, or working for change in services, (c) working for change in his or her own agency, or (d) being a policy conduit for change, meaning being an expert in an area and providing education on needed changes to policymakers. Wyers concluded by stating that "all social workers need to participate in the modification of social policy that is harmful to clients and the elimination of policy deficits by working for new policy" (Wyers, 1991, p. 246). McInnis-Dittrich (1994) agreed that the meaning of professional social work, by definition, means integrating social welfare policy and social work practice.

However, most definitions of policy practice are largely defined by interventions designed to change policies in legislative, agency, or community settings from a largely macro practice perspective. Figueira-McDonough (1993) defines policy practice as the formal process of influencing both legislative and judicial decision making, as well as constituency-based patterns of influence in communities and organizations. She outlines four methods of policy practice in these arenas: legislative advocacy, reform through litigation, social action, and policy analysis. Jansson (2003) defines policy practice as efforts to change policies in legislative, agency, and community settings. He further differentiates policy advocacy from policy practice by stating that policy advocacy focuses on performing policy practice methods with powerless groups, to improve their resources and opportunities. However, he admits that he uses the terms interchangeably throughout much of his discussion.

A related term, which has been used repeatedly in the literature is, *political social work*. Political social work has been defined differently depending on the author. In a discussion of these differing definitions, Fisher (1995) suggested that "policy implementation, electoral activity, community organizing—macro methods—were what most people in the profession understood as political social work" (p. 198). This approach to political social work focuses largely on a more traditional sense of politics, such as "legislation, the executive branch, interest groups, lobbying, working with the media, and running for office" (Hoefer, 1999, p. 75). Contrary to this approach is a more integrated approach that sees all social work as political social work, regardless of what level of practice, micro or macro, one focuses her or his interventions. For this integrated approach, political social work is seen as social work based on a politicized understanding of social welfare, and methods of practice are integrated. Thus, the goal is to train politicized social workers who see issues of power and justice as central to understanding and addressing social problems, as well as confronting client needs.

Many authors have used the term *advocacy* in their definition of what I consider policy practice skills. Let me first emphasize that advocacy related to policy practice must be distinguished from case advocacy because of the systemic nature of the change. For example, if a social worker has a client who experiences a problem maneuvering through the maze of social programs and we assist her or him in gaining resources, then we are performing case advocacy. But if we see client after client having the same problem, then it becomes a waste of valuable time and resources to individually advocate for each client. That is when policy practice comes into play. We want to advocate making a policy change so that all of the clients can receive these services, and we do not have the time to advocate for each one of them individually. It is time to perform policy practice.

But even within the description of class advocacy, there is a rather complex array of definitions of various attributes of advocacy. For example, Schneider and Lester (2001) differentiate in great detail their definition of advocacy as the "mutual representation of a client or clients or a cause in a forum, attempting to systematically influence decision making in an unjust or unresponsive system[s]" (p. 65) from other forms of social work practice. For example, they suggest that advocacy is a form of social action, incorporating many of the concepts of system level change and influence, but it is specifically responsible to a client or client system in a forum within an exclusive and mutual relationship. Distinguishing their definition from community organizing (CO), they state that CO is primarily an organizing and capacity-building function with emphasis on collective support through education and participation to address common concerns.

Ezell (2001) created a typology of different forms of advocacy, indicating that there was actually little variation in their meaning, although scholars have seemed to have a preference for one or the other on a theoretical level. He includes class advocacy, an intervention on behalf of a group of clients who share the same problem; systems advocacy, changing policies and practices affecting all persons in a certain group; policy advocacy, efforts to influence those who work with laws, public programs, or court decisions; political advocacy, which appears the same as class, policy, and systems advocacy; legislative advocacy, promoting and influencing legislation; and community advocacy, organizing and educating on behalf of communities who have similar problems or needs but may not be known to each other.

It is academically important to build theories and methods around various policy practice and advocacy definitions. Rapid Reference 1.1 summarizes the various concepts of what we have included under the larger

≡ Rapid Reference 1.1

Concepts Used to Describe Policy-Related Social Work

Policy practice	Legislative advocacy
Policy advocacy	Reform through litigation
Political advocacy	Policy analysis
Political social work	Social action
Class advocacy	Community organizing
System advocacy	Community development

rubric of political social work. Much of this work targets advocacy at the legislative, judicial, community, and agency settings. It also largely differentiates itself from community techniques of community organizing, community development, and social action (with the exception of Figueira-McDonough). For the purposes of skill building, it is important to use whatever techniques work for a given problem with a given population. And while I think the theory building that has occurred at the academic level of policy practice and advocacy is important, I am more interested in pursuing the next level of how to reach the goals to change a system that needs to be changed, and learning to use whatever skills are necessary and appropriate to make those changes occur. The goal of this book, therefore, is to move away from theoretical and conceptual discussions of policy practice and focus on the skill sets necessary to put it into practice. In some instances, methods and skills of community work are necessarily integrated into more traditional views of policy practice, because mobilizing the community is part of how to reach people, and people are needed in order to work in policy practice at a grassroots level.

WHY COMMUNITY-BASED POLICY PRACTICE?

In this book, policy practice encompasses all of the work that social workers do to try to change systems for the betterment of their clients, neighborhoods, and communities. The focus in this book, however, is on the specific skills needed to change policy from a community-based, grassroots perspective. While most policy practice is discussed in the realm of the larger political system, there is a need to look at policy practice from the ground up. Policy at all levels affects people, their neighborhoods, and their local communities. Regardless of where the policy originates, be it local government, a school system, an agency, the county, the state, or in the courts, it ultimately affects individual people. Oftentimes we believe that policy is too large, too complex, and too removed from the people for us to be able to have an influence. But the fact is that most policy that affects our day-to-day lives is very much within the realm of our influence.

After 12 years of working with various task groups on specific local, state, and federal policies, it has become abundantly clear that with the proper planning and skills, a small group of motivated people can make major changes that can positively impact entire communities. There are generic skills that can be used to target any system of change, including mobilizing the community around an issue, using the media to inform both the public and decision makers of problems or policy solutions, and using technology to get the word out to as many people as possible about issues that need to be addressed. Other skills are more particular to a certain target system, such as testifying before local and state committees or participating in grassroots campaign movements. The point is that individuals and members of local communities are very powerful in influencing the decisions that affect our daily lives, regardless of the level of government or bureaucracy from which they stem. But we need a skill set, a way to plan the changes to make them effective, and an understanding of who to target to make the change, and that is the primary focus of this book.

POLICY PRACTICE IN THE COMMUNITY AS A RESPONSE TO DEVOLUTION

This book emphasizes the community as a good beginning point to do many different types of policy practice. It is important to understand how the political climate has changed over the last 20 years that makes it more important to target local levels of government and to use grassroots approaches to target higher and more distant public officials. Linhorst (2002) recounts the history of federalism, which has given way to the decentralization of decision making to the local and state levels of government. Federalism is a system of government that divides responsibilities of governing among various levels of government. In the United States, responsibilities have traditionally been divided horizontally across the executive, legislative, and judicial branches, but also vertically among the federal, state, and local levels of government. In his historical account of federalism in this country, Linhorst explains that prior to the Great

Depression U.S. federalism was characterized by dual federalism, where clear roles were assigned to the federal and state governments, with states holding considerable power. Cooperative federalism developed after the Depression, however, because state governments needed assistance in response to adverse economic conditions. Federal power and control over programs increased drastically during this time.

Throughout the 1960s cooperative dualism existed in this country, until the current state of federalism was initiated by President Nixon. Believing that the federal government had grown too large, he provided block grants and general revenue-sharing dollars to local governments, increased uniformity in the food stamp program across states, and initiated supplemental security income. This state of federalism was dubbed "New" federalism. It did not decrease revenues to the state, but gave them more flexibility to create programs that were locally appropriate. But President Reagan took the concept of new federalism to another level, by supporting less government at all levels, devolving federal power to the states, and at the same time cutting federal social programs and reducing funds originally targeted to state and local governments. The 104th Congress (mid-1990s) took devolution even further by seeking to eliminate federal entitlement programs, reducing overall federal spending even further, and cutting taxes at the same time. Although most of the responsibility for implementing social programs has now shifted to the states, the federal government continues to be the primary funder. Much of the decision-making authority now rests with state and local governments, making it easier for agencies to create their own rules and regulations based on local mandates. Thus, the decision-making authority is much closer to home.

The social work literature is replete with research on how the way devolution has been handled has hurt the poor, decreased protection of oppressed populations, and increased the inequities in social protection between the states. However, devolution also had the consequence of bringing much of the power base and decision making back to state and local governments. Whereas in the past, policy practitioners spent much of their time working at the federal level of government, the changing nature of federalism requires social workers to adapt their policy practice to the state and local levels. One of the consequences of the new federalism is that although few initiatives have been enacted by the federal government that have helped our constituents, considerable gains have been made at the state level. Unfortunately, the research does not indicate that the new federalism has helped promote social equity or justice at the local levels, yet federal oversight is still needed to ensure that local communities meet the needs of their citizens.

With the state of new federalism, it is unlikely that the federal government is willing to provide much oversight for citizen protection. However, because many problems are community based, meaning that the problems—and often the solutions—can be found in our own communities, social workers are in a unique position to hold local communities responsible as well. As Linhorst (2002) points out, "the current phase of new federalism has devolved increased responsibility to the states, and social workers, as we have done historically, need to adapt our approach to promoting social justice" (p. 205). What social workers need is the knowledge and skills to be able to identify problems, seek out alternative solutions, and make changes that can assist as many community members as possible. Although interventions at the federal level are still important, it is an opportune time to turn our attention to state and local policies because they now have much of the decision-making authority. They are closer to home, are easier to communicate with, have a better understanding of the local problems that we encounter, and have an increased likelihood of successful policy interventions at a more local level.

POLICY PRACTICE AND THE ETHICS OF THE PROFESSION

The code of ethics is quite clear on our responsibility as a profession to perform policy practice activities. The ethical responsibility of social workers to engage in social and political change efforts is clearly set out in section 6.04a of the National Association of Social Workers' Code of Ethics (1999):

> Social workers should engage in social and political action that seeks to ensure that all people have equal access to the resources, employment, services, and opportunities they require to meet their basic human needs and to develop fully. Social workers should be aware of the impact of the political arena on practice and should advocate for changes in policy and legislation to improve social conditions in order to meet basic human needs and promote social justice.

There are six principles in the code of ethics from which the standards derive. Rapid Reference 1.2 delineates the six principles in the code. Once we realize the importance of advocating on the part of our clients, neighbors, and communities, it becomes clear that each of these six principles has something to do with policy practice. For example, principle 1 states that the primary goal is to help people in need and to address social problems. But how can we really address social problems if we do not practice

---

≡ Rapid Reference 1.2

Ethical Principles in the Code of Ethics of the National Association of Social Workers (1999)

1. Social workers' primary goal is to help people in need and to address social problems.
2. Social workers challenge social injustice.
3. Social workers respect the inherent dignity and worth of the person.
4. Social workers recognize the central importance of human relationships.
5. Social workers behave in a trustworthy manner.
6. Social workers practice within their areas of competence and develop and enhance their professional expertise.

policy? A personal problem becomes a social problem when it affects a large number of people. If a problem is affecting a large number of people, then something is amiss. Either a community is having economic problems of some sort that are affecting a large number of people, a policy that is supposed to support families is not working properly, or an agency that is supposed to supply a certain service is not functioning effectively. All of these issues point to a target system that needs an intervention of some sort. This is policy practice.

The goal of social justice as part of both the social work code of ethics and our profession's person-in-environment perspective has been a challenge for social workers. Although social work as a profession has made a commitment to social justice for the families we work with, social workers are often challenged because they lack skills in the strategies and techniques of policy practice needed to realize policy change. As Gordon (1994) points out, by not taking a leadership role in the formulation and implementation of the policies that affect our clients, the profession's person-in-environment perspective is largely missing from programs and services. Learning policy practice methods and skills is seen as a "necessary means to the implementation of the neglected goal of social justice" (Figueira-McDonough, 1993, p. 180). The integration of policy practice methods emphasizing social and organizational change with direct practice content is a challenge. But this integration is essential to broaden the influence that social service workers have to promote positive impacts in our clients' lives.

DOES POLICY PRACTICE REALLY WORK?

Many people, and social workers are no exception, feel helpless to try to make changes in the systems we work with, whether it is in our own agency or in a legislative body. But this book provides evidence that, with good planning and the right skill sets, changes can and do occur. The methods outlined in this book have been utilized since 1992 with social work students, and the results have been impressive (Rocha & Johnson, 1997).

Throughout this book, examples of projects that have both prevailed and failed are given, with tips on why they did or did not work.

This book is an outgrowth of not only years of teaching, but also evaluating whether the planning model works. In 2000, graduates who had taken the course and had formed task groups and used the skills in this book to try to make changes in their communities were surveyed 6 months after graduation. These graduates were compared with graduates who had taken other advanced policy practice courses, but did not have the experience of going into the community and using the planned change method (Rocha, 2000). The study assessed three dimensions of policy-related activities: (a) whether policy practice activities were valued as important tasks, (b) whether graduates felt competent in doing policy practice activities, and (c) how active the graduates were in actually performing policy practice activities since they graduated. All graduates reported valuing policy practice equally. Those with policy practice experience were significantly more likely to feel competent using the media to communicate ideas to the public, plan and implement a planned change effort, use the Internet to find policy-related information, and create computer-generated information (e.g., brochures, newsletters). Students who had policy practice experience were also significantly more likely to have worked on a specific change effort since graduation, become a member of a committee or coalition, and were more likely to organize policy activities. Thus, whether a student or practitioner, I urge the reader to put the ideas in this book to use. Activities at the end of each chapter provide added opportunities for practice.

This book provides a policy practice planning process that is familiar to both community social workers and clinicians alike because it uses similar steps as the problem-solving models that are often used with individual clients. It provides step-by-step instructions on how to put a plan into action. Each chapter describes detailed skills that can be used to bring awareness to problems, utilize resources to deal with problems, and put into action a plan to solve the problems. Many skills can be used at several levels, from local community issues, such as transportation and child care, to larger issues, such as changing laws to create more equitable distribution of resources. Each chapter presents new skill sets, depending on the system requiring change. There are many examples and illustrations, in the hope that the more we practice these skills, the more competent we feel to utilize them.

The next chapter outlines the planning stage in great detail. The following four chapters detail specific skill sets that can be used across targeted systems for change (e.g., utilizing the media, organizing coalitions). The last four chapters look at different potential target systems and provide in-depth information on particular strategies needed to intervene within these systems (e.g., local agencies, legislature). Thus, some skills are specific to a particular target system, but many of the skills from the previous chapters can be used across targeted systems. The important thing to remember is that each problem and each strategy should be analyzed carefully to assess what will likely lead to the best outcome for your clients.

SUMMARY

In an age of devolution of both resources and decision making down to the local level, social workers have greater opportunities to effect change, but also increased challenges, due to decreased resources. Policy practice skills are necessary to address these challenges and seize opportunities to make substantial differences in the lives of our clients. The skills and target systems discussed in the next chapters will provide easy-to-follow instructions on how to strategize changes in many different systems.

 TEST YOURSELF

1. Provide one example of how the ethical principle of "respecting the inherent dignity and worth of the person" could be linked to policy practice.

2. Identify a social problem of interest to you. Trace backward the assistance that people are given. Where does the funding come from?

3. Identify a policy that an agency you are affiliated with has. Where does the policy originate? Is it formal or informal?

4. Think about a specific client group that you work with. What are some of the problems they face? Do several clients face the same problems?

5. Remember the discussion on the difference between case and class advocacy. How different would it be to try to solve a problem for an entire group of clients, rather than one at a time?

6. Why has the goal of social justice in the profession's "person-in-environment perspective" been such a challenge for social workers?

7. Discuss the opportunities and challenges of devolution.

8. How has devolution impacted the way social workers must work in the policy practice arena?

9. Policy practice methods can be used at the local level as well as the federal level. True or False?

10. Policy practice methods should only be used in the legislative arena and are inappropriate for use in judicial decision making. True or False?

Answers: 9. True; 10. False

Two

ESSENTIALS OF THE PLANNING PROCESS

The planning process is an essential feature of policy practice. Planning is crucial at each stage of the change effort and should flow from an in-depth understanding of the problem, the policy, and others who are working on the issue. Likewise, the actual strategy of change should flow from broad goals, measurable objectives, and specific tactics and techniques designed to carry out the plan. Finally, the implementation should be flexible enough to change as circumstances in the environment change. Including an evaluation component during and after implementation will make a feedback loop where flexibility is possible.

Planning is important in any planned change effort, whether you are working on a public awareness campaign, working with local agencies, running an election campaign, or working on state legislative issues. Throughout this book, the planning process is used again and again. One must plan, strategize, implement, evaluate, and then revise the plan, based on feedback from the effort. Research on community awareness campaigns, running for local elections, strategizing legislative advocacy, and creating internal organizational change has all stressed planning as the linchpin for success. Just as the policy practice planning process is similar to the problem-solving approach utilized in direct practice with clients, it can also be used to plan the approach to a variety of community-level interventions. Rapid Reference 2.1 introduces the five-step planning process that will be used throughout this book.

≡ Rapid Reference 2.1

Policy Practice Planning Process

I. Problem identification
   A. Describe problem
   B. Analyze problem and the corresponding policy
   C. Identify target system for change
II. Advocacy intervention plan
   A. What is the broad goal of the advocacy effort?
   B. What measurable objectives have you chosen?
III. Possible intervention strategies/tactics/activities—for each objective, list several interventions with:
   A. Advantages (resources available)
   B. Disadvantages (obstacles anticipated) for each
   C. Interventions chosen
   D. Rationale
IV. Implementation
V. Evaluation

PROBLEM IDENTIFICATION

The first stage of the policy practice method is to assess the problem. What is known and not known about the problem? Who is affected by the problem and how are they affected? It is important to first identify the problem before the policy is identified. A thorough understanding of the problem will be a guide toward a better understanding of the policy. To analyze the problem in detail, there is an abundance of resources that can be used, depending on whether the problem is local or is on a larger systemic level. Therefore, the first step is to assess who is being affected. It is possible it is a community problem at the local level, an agency problem for a specific group of clients, or a larger problem that affects everyone in a given county, state, or country. Even if it seems like a very large problem, it may be possible to intervene at a smaller systems level. For example, although the minimum wage is far below the poverty level for most families, many states have set a minimum wage that is higher than the federal level. Many cities have set a living wage that is higher than either the state or the federal minimum wage. So it is important to identify the problem and then begin to analyze what policies are present or absent that are designed to address it.

The second step is to analyze what policy is designed to address the problem. This is a very important task, and one that requires attention to detail. For example, although an agency may have a policy that does not address the needs of a certain population, they may or may not be the target for change. It is important to find out whether the problem is at the agency level, whether it is a regulatory requirement, or whether there is a law governing what the agency must do. This step will guide the policy practitioner, task force, or coalition toward their target for change. Rapid Reference 2.2 provides some resources that can be used to obtain statistics at several levels of government (McInniss-Dittrich, 1994), as well as where one might begin to look for the policy that determines the target system.

Once the problem and the policy behind it are well understood, it is time to assess the past and current attempts that have been used to address the problem and what some of the barriers have been to alleviate it. There is no sense in duplicating either what has been tried and failed in the past, or what another group may be working on simultaneously. The first step is to look at what has been tried in the past. Who tried it? What was the political climate at the time? Analyzing past efforts to address problems or change policies is important. What did not work in the past might indeed work in the present. Agencies, administrators, legislators, and school board members all change. Because of this, timing is very important, and a good analysis of past attempts and why they did not work is vital.

Current attempts to address the problem are also important. If there are already groups or organizations working on an issue, they can join forces together or tackle the problem from different angles. But what we do not

≡ Rapid Reference 2.2

Resources

Where to Find Statistics to Show Evidence of a Problem	Potential Targets for Policy Change
Sources for local statistics	*Targets for local systems*
Media (newspapers, radio, and TV)	City government
Census Bureau	County government
Grassroots/neighborhood groups	School board
The Internet	Planning commission
Local library	Transit Authority
City/county data books	Department of Human Services
Public hearings	Public health department
Public agencies	Police department
Agency newsletters	Nonprofit agencies
Sources for State- and Federal-Level Statistics	*Targets for State- and Federal-Level Policies*
Census Bureau	Legislators
State home page	Governor/President
Internet	Executive branch agencies, such as Department of Education
Policy institutes	
Bureau of Labor Statistics	Department of Health
Library databases	Department of Children's Services
General Accounting Office (GAO)	Housing and Urban Development (HUD)
Media	
Public agencies (DHHS, HUD, etc.)	Judicial appointments

want to do is to duplicate each others' efforts, or worse yet, undermine what others are doing. Both of these steps allow the practitioner to assess what the barriers to meeting the needs are by virtue of the experiences of others who have tried to make changes.

Thus, the first stage is an information-gathering stage, which helps define the problem, identify the policy source, and assess what has been tried and what is currently being tried to solve the problem. After this first step is completed and a thorough understanding of all aspects of the problem are understood, it is time to establish goals and objectives and begin to plan the intervention.

ADVOCACY INTERVENTION PLAN

The second step of the planning process is to establish one major goal for the advocacy effort. Why just one goal? Because goals are broad statements about what we would like to see as the outcome. Goals are general statements about what we would like to achieve. Each goal will be broken down into measurable objectives and those objectives will be broken down into specific strategies and tactics that will be used to achieve the overall goal. While having only one goal may seem too small, once the planning continues it becomes apparent that there is much to be done, even for one goal.

After the goal is established it is important to be able to break it down into measurable objectives. Generally, one goal should not have more than one or two objectives. Objectives are more specific than goals. They should be attainable, measurable, and lead to the goal.

Possible Intervention Strategies

After each objective is established, alternative ways to fulfill those objectives should be explored, considering as many strategies to solve the problem as possible, using available resources and developing new ones. This stage also includes thinking through the consequences of the proposed alternatives. It is important to recognize that there are always consequences to alternatives, both intended and unintended. Since we first and foremost want to do no harm to our clients, this stage must be analyzed intently. When thinking through alterna-

> **CAUTION**
>
> Don't forget to brainstorm potential obstacles and unanticipated consequences of all alternative strategies.

tive strategies to fulfill objectives, first brainstorm all the different tactics and strategies that would fulfill the objective. Then for each tactic, think about the advantages and disadvantages of each one. What resources are there to fulfill the strategy? Anticipate obstacles, think of potential unintended consequences, and brainstorm potential barriers.

Choose the interventions that have the least costs and the most potential benefits. This may seem obvious to the reader, but the planning process is essential, and it's best to write it all down. Once a group begins brainstorming alternatives and potential pros and cons of each, issues such as resources, time constraints, politics, and so on come to the forefront. So often groups begin the planning stage with a problem and go straight to an action plan—but it is the steps in the middle that will ensure that the plan is solid, hasn't already been attempted, isn't being duplicated, and that all potential negative consequences have been thought out. Sometimes the most interesting or dramatic plans have to be reworked because of potential negative consequences to clients. In one case in Cleveland, for example, a student group trying to assist public-assistance clients with their managed health care plan thought of a dramatic strategy to march the clients to the managed-care organization for a mass disenrollment (in Ohio at that time, clients could choose managed care or traditional Medicaid). They planned to get good media attention and hoped that it would bring attention to the plight of the managed-care recipients. After careful research of the policy, however, they found that there was a waiting period between managed care and Medicaid of several weeks. It was determined that it would put too many families at risk in case of an emergency during the waiting period and an alternative plan was chosen (Rocha & Johnson, 1997). Although the new plan was not as sexy, it was a trade-off for the safety and welfare of the clients' families.

The following Putting It Into Practice gives a good example of how the planning process takes place. Notice that the broad goal for this task force was simply to extend the bus route so that clients without transportation to an organization would be able to access agency services. In the example, the objectives were to create awareness of the dangers of not having the bus route extended and to create support for the bus line extension. These are much more specific than the goal, but if carried out, should lead to the goal being met. In this instance the target organization was the Transit Authority. But as shown in the planning process, this simple task required more than one objective and even more tactics before it could become a reality.

In the present example, the transportation task force brainstormed several possible strategies to attain their goal before deciding on these particular tactics. They thought of eliciting letters from families telling their stories of the dangers of walking the 2 miles from the last bus stop to the agency. The advantage of this would have been that those individuals directly affected would have a voice in the process. However, this strategy would also have compromised client confidentiality. Thus, they felt that having the needs assessment conducted by agency personnel maintained client confidentiality but also provided anecdotal evidence to meet their first objective.

The task force also brainstormed other approaches to get greater public support for the change. They considered launching a public awareness campaign and utilizing media attention. The advantages of this strategy would have been both greater public support and pressure on the transportation agency to accept their proposal. But the disadvantages were that the transportation board would likely see this tactic as highly oppositional and become resistant to change. Furthermore, the task force had already established a relationship with the Service Development Director, who had shown an interest in collaborating with the group, and they did not

Putting It Into Practice

Example of the Planning Process

Describing the problem: A local agency was set up to meet the therapeutic needs of children of sexual abuse. But the clinicians noticed that many people were late for their appointments and there were many no-shows. The therapists began to ask the parents what their needs were in order to be able to make their appointments. A recurring theme was that many families did not have transportation and relied on the bus system to access the facility. However, the bus stopped almost a half mile up the road and families were forced to walk the rest of the way on a busy street with no sidewalks, children in tow.

Analyzing the policy: After a bit of investigation, it was found that the transportation route was an artifact of an old mapping system that had not kept up with the current growth in businesses in that area.

Identifying the target system for change: A graduate student who was interning at the agency offered to plan a change effort to see if the transit system would extend the bus line by 2.7 miles. Although this would seem a simple task, the transit system, like any bureaucratic agency, would be resistant to change without very compelling evidence to make a decision, mainly because of the extra resources that would be needed to extend the route without evidence that it would be economically feasible to do so. The student formed a task group for the sole purpose of changing the bus route. Their group investigated the problem to find out how many families were actually impacted by the half-mile hike to the facility, and how many children were involved. They also targeted the transit system only after researching where the rule originated, finding that the transit system had the authority to change the policy if they determined it was economically feasible to do so.

Goal: Having researched the problem and policy, and determining the target system, they decided their broad goal would be to extend the transit route to pass by the agency.

Objectives: Their first objective was to create awareness within the transit authority of the dangers of not having transportation on that end of the major thoroughfare. Because there were other businesses in the area that would benefit from the increased bus service, they decided a second objective would be to obtain the support of businesses in the area to further the route.

(continued)

Possible intervention strategies: The task group looked at several alternative strategies and tactics that might enable them to convince the transit authorities that it would be cost effective and feasible to change the route. To meet the first objective, they conducted a needs assessment from families who used the agency, with their stories of the dangers of walking on the road. To meet the second objective, they surveyed the existing businesses to estimate how many potential riders there might be if the bus went a full mile to the new shopping center that had just been opened, which contained a large grocery store and several restaurants. They also elicited letters of support from businesses in the area. They designed a map of a potential new route and contacted the transit system to find out when their next meeting would be in order to get on the agenda to speak to the transit board.

Implementation: They were put on the agenda and produced their new bus route, their statistics on increased ridership, their stories from families detailing their experiences, and letters from businesses supporting the proposed expansion. The task force was met with polite recognition that they would look at the evidence and make a decision before the next meeting, but the general manager gave them his verbal support of the project. The group left the meeting unsure if their strategy would work.

Evaluation: During the ensuing weeks they evaluated their efforts and brainstormed alternative plans in case their original plan failed. They were thrilled to learn within a couple of weeks that, indeed, the transit board decided to invest the money to expand the route. The transit authority also requested members of the task force to remain as a liaison between the social service agency and the transit authority.

want to alienate that contact. This story illustrates the complexities of the planning process and how each step must be analyzed, and the advantages and disadvantages of potential strategies thoroughly examined.

Implementation and Evaluation

Throughout the plan's implementation, the objectives must be evaluated and repeatedly reevaluated for effectiveness. Both process objectives, which are the ways the plan is being carried out, and outcome objectives should be discussed and evaluated. Evaluation is essential because as with any problem-solving process, there is a feedback loop that must be evident, so that if a strategy is not working, the evaluation mechanism will catch it and the objectives or tactics can be revisited.

DON'T FORGET

Every stage of the planning process is important and builds onto the next step. If you leave out a step, you may find yourself duplicating something that has already been done, or something already tried and failed.

In the example provided in this chapter the task force was prepared for implementation. They were able to show the dangers families experienced by not having the bus route extended, as well as the increase in ridership that would occur from the extension. The two-pronged approach was effective, because it did not just ask the transportation agency to feel sorry for people, but showed how cost effective it would be because of increased revenues from the local area businesses. And to make sure that the route went to the needed areas, the task group even added a map, both with the existing route and the expanded route.

At times, when we get to implementation and evaluation, we feel our planning process is complete. But for effective implementation it is a good idea to use great detail. A Program Evaluation and Review Technique (PERT) chart is a good way to plan the implementation and evaluation phase. It can be used to make sure that the final stage of the planning session is thoughtfully carried out. The following steps are used in PERT:

1. Describe final steps in implementation.
2. Outline all events that must occur (phone calls, visits, putting together material, and so forth).
3. Order these steps chronologically.
4. List all activities, resources, and materials needed for each step.
5. Estimate the time needed to accomplish each activity by the deadline.

6. Determine who will be responsible for each task by assigning people according to the time they have to accomplish the task by the deadline (Galanes, Adams, & Brilhart, 2004).

This planning process can be used with any target system. On a local level, it can be used with local bureaucratic agencies, nonprofits, school systems, city councils, or to bring public awareness to an issue. The Putting It Into Practice exercise in this chapter is one of many examples that will be given throughout the book on various strategies and target systems. Depending on the target system, some tactics are better than others. For example, the task force that wanted to change the bus route was brainstorming other intervention strategies while they waited to see if their first approach worked. They thought of bringing media attention to the issue, putting a bit more pressure on the transit authority. But these were unnecessary because their first strategies were successful. Conversely, in other situations, the use of the media would not necessarily be used to put pressure on an entity but rather bring public awareness to an issue. So, it actually depends on the target system and the goal of the policy practice effort as to the appropriate interventions to be used.

The rest of this book will look more closely at various intervention strategies and explore which skills are most appropriate with which target system. The next four chapters will discuss several strategies and skills in detail that can be used across target systems. Their usefulness in different contexts will be thoroughly explained. The final four chapters will focus on specific target systems and will use both strategies specific to those systems as well as discuss the utility of the more generic strategies in Chapters 3 through 6. One of the caveats of structuring the book in this way is that we have a tendency to jump into a problem and choose a strategy to fix things without proper planning up front. I can tell you from experience that this is not a good idea. First, inaccurate or superficial analysis of the problem leads to strategies that will likely fail, for a variety of reasons. By not assessing who else is working on the problem, you may waste time duplicating others' efforts. By not assessing what has already been tried, you may propose a solution that is already being implemented (I've seen this happen and it's quite embarrassing). Second, not giving the potential target system a careful analysis may result in wasting precious time and resources. Targeting an agency for change, for example, when its hands are tied by a legislative mandate is, at best, a waste of time, and at worse, it hurts the credibility of your group.

But the advantage of learning a variety of skills and techniques for change up front is that many of these can be used effectively across target systems. Thus a thorough understanding of these skills, and when to use them, is essential when reading the last four chapters, which focus on targeting change in communities, agencies, legislative bodies, and the judicial system. By having a good skill base, the later chapters generate more ideas of appropriate use of strategies and increase the likelihood that the reader can quickly and critically assess which skills are needed for a given problem. The caution is, then, not to jump the gun and bypass the planning process. It is not an academic exercise; it is a real-life necessity for success to be realized when trying to make important changes.

SUMMARY

This chapter provides a description of the planning process that is vital to any policy practice effort. It is an extension of the problem-solving model used in direct practice and, thus, should be familiar to most social workers. It includes identifying the problem, analyzing the policy, identifying the target system of the planned change effort, and goal setting—prioritizing objectives and strategizing which tactics and techniques will likely solve the problem. Looking at potential obstacles and resources is very important in the planning process, particularly when brainstorming strategies for change. Identifying who else might be working on the issue is also essential, to avoid duplicating or undermining another group's efforts. Finally, having an evaluation method that allows for continuous evaluation of what is working and what may not be working is important for flexibility and being able to loop back and make changes along the way.

TEST YOURSELF

Group Exercise. Choose one of the following problems and think about how you would find information about the problem and the policy. Where might you look for statistics to provide evidence that your problem affects more than just a few people? What resources could you use to find the corresponding policy? For each, who would be a likely target for a policy practice intervention? Think of what goal you would like to see occur that would ameliorate the problem. Break your goal down into one or two specific objectives.

1. You have noticed that a large number of people that get off welfare tend to be back on within 2 years.

2. There is an increase in the number of incidences at your public high school of gay and lesbian teens being harassed.

3. There have been reports at your women's shelter that the police are not responding to domestic violence calls.

4. It seems that there has been an influx of mentally ill persons incarcerated in your county.

5. The Department of Health has extra flu vaccines this year, but due to an earlier report that there would not be enough vaccine for all who needed it, people are not coming to the clinic to be vaccinated.

6. The state legislature is debating a law that would make it illegal for gay and lesbian couples to adopt children.

7. The local school system has instituted strict zero-tolerance policies, resulting in a substantial increase in suspensions and expulsions of students. The alternative school is full and many students are simply staying home.

8. The city planning commission has decided to allow a developer to build a strip mall in an area of the city that expanded substantially over the last few years. The mall will be located on a previously protected watershed.

9. The city has received a federal grant to tear down a large public housing project and replace it with low to moderately priced single-family dwellings, potentially displacing hundreds of low-income residents.

10. Elderly residents in your community must walk five blocks to access the nearest bus line.

Remember, don't try to think of specific intervention strategies right now—these will be covered in great detail in the forthcoming chapters. For now, it is important to be able to distinguish between problems, policies, and target systems, and to distinguish between a broad goal and specific objectives.

Three

ESSENTIALS OF EFFECTIVE INTERPERSONAL COMMUNICATION AND PARTICIPATION

All of the potential goals, objectives, and strategies that were discussed in Chapter 2 have one thing in common: people. It is important to understand the skills needed to interact with people in many different areas. If we are working with the media, we must successfully create relationships with editors, reporters, producers, and interviewers. When we work in the community, we must be able to listen to and understand the frustration of citizens, even if their circumstances, cultures, and lifestyles are very different from our own. Working in agency settings requires good interpersonal communication skills. When we work in the legislative arena, relationships are probably the most important asset we have. We must convey integrity, honesty, and knowledge of our issues. Enhancing our ability to empathize, listen, participate rather than dictate, and learn to effectively facilitate process will go a long way in almost any policy practice project and in almost any target system.

Although there are many skills involved in policy practice, how we convey our message is just as important as who gets the message. Skills in facilitation, communication (both oral and written), conveying integrity and honesty, relationship-building, and being able to critically analyze complex problems and situations are the hallmark of good social work. These are also some of the most important skills that cut across all policy practice situations. While the bulk of this chapter will address the use of interpersonal skills in garnering grassroots participation in the policy process, I want to first discuss how these skills cut across all aspects of policy practice.

Whether we are working for change in the legislature, with agencies, or the judicial system, the way we interact with others has much to do with our credibility, and our power to persuade others to change policies and programs. I have often heard decision makers talk about credibility and integrity as being the most important attributes influencing their decisions on policy matters. Legislators, for example, receive much of their information from lobbyists to help them make decisions on thousands of bills that come through the legislature each year. Their reputation rests on the integrity of that information. If legislators feel misled, lobbyists lose their credibility.

Likewise, when task groups and coalitions attempt to make changes in organizations at the local level, it is extremely important to build relationships with decision makers in those organizations. Hoefer (2006) asserts that the amount of persuasion that people have with decision makers depends on how one is perceived. Perceptions are based on expertise, good communications skills, honesty, and trust that is built over time.

Rose (1999, p. 10) discusses how basic social work skills create successful policy practitioners and links the two skill sets in some interesting ways. The following are some of the linkages that Rose sees in how basic social work skills interface with the policy practice process:

- Social workers' ability to demonstrate objectivity, to think in highly charged, emotional environments; keeping to a position that is well thought out while remaining open to new information is also critical in political discourse.
- The *disciplined use of self* emphasized in clinical social work practice is an invaluable skill for the successful municipal leader.
- The social work orientation of considering multiple causes and sources of stress and resources in making an assessment is congruent with the principles of democratic government and its impact on a variety of constituent groups.
- While effective verbal communication, active listening, and cooperation are essential for participation in legislative meetings

and for maintaining connection with constituents, legislators do not always have specific training in these communications skills. Social workers do!

INTERPERSONAL SKILLS FOR GRASSROOTS PARTICIPATION

In almost every change effort, people power is essential to change, because there is power in numbers. Policy practice can rarely be effective without community involvement and support. Communities know their problems better than anyone. With an understanding of the systems that help assist or undermine their wellbeing, they will also know the potential solutions to their problems. The task of the policy practitioner, therefore, must also include community practice skills that encourage community involvement. Without the grassroots voice of communities, decision makers will not know whether their constituents really support many of the potential policies that may help the community. Although community members know best what their problems and needs are, they are also often disenfranchised from the very system that has the power to make decisions that could alleviate some of their problems. This disenfranchisement presents itself in apathy, lack of trust of the process, and a feeling that what they do will not matter. The task of the community practitioner is to facilitate a process of empowerment that allows people to understand that they can make a difference and educate them on ways to make changes. In this respect, using community practice principles for interpersonal communication is essential to produce the kinds of grassroots support needed for effective policy practice outcomes.

At this point the reader may be wondering what the differences are between community practitioners and policy practitioners. As we discussed in Chapter 1, policy practice is largely defined by interventions designed to change policies in legislative, agency, or community settings. Community practice, on the other hand, is defined by the *Encyclopedia of Social Work* as "multiple methods of empowerment-based interventions to strengthen participation in democratic processes, assist groups and communities in advocating for their needs and organizing for social justice, and to improve the effectiveness and responsiveness of human service systems"(Weil & Gamble, 1995, p. 577). While policy practice theoretically can be done without the involvement of community, it is unwise to perceive policy practice so narrowly. There are numerous examples, some of which we will discuss in this chapter, that indicate that without grassroots support of policy initiatives, policy change is difficult to achieve. So while policy practice takes on a more advocacy role to change policy to assist people, community practice gets real involvement from the ground up through community participation. But community participation is not something that just happens. Increasing community participation requires skills in and of itself because many communities do not feel that their involvement will make a difference. The apathy among citizens in this country overall is extremely high, as evidenced by voter turnout. Only 50 percent of all eligible voters voted in the 2000 presidential election and 56 percent in the 2004 election (Federal Election Commission, 2004; OECD, 2001). The turnout for local elections is even smaller. As one can surmise, if we cannot even get out the vote, how can we expect that people will organize around issues of concern unless there is some way that people feel that their voice matters? Given this situation, the complementarity between policy practice and community practice is essential, and policy practitioners must use community practice skills to organize grassroots support around issues of importance to the community. Much of the skill base needed to work with communities is grounded in generalist and individual practice social work skills of interpersonal helping. Rapid Reference 3.1 shows the intersection of skills needed.

While these are only a few of the interpersonal skills needed in policy practice, it is fairly obvious that part of the skills needed are basic social work communication skills: respect for diversity, listening skills, and problem identification skills. The difference is that these skills are used with groups of people rather than with one person at a time. Also very important is the acknowledgment that we are not the experts on others'

≡ *Rapid Reference 3.1*

Skills Needed for Interpersonal Grassroots Policy Practice

Individual Interpersonal Helping Skills

- Self awareness in facilitating individual change—sensitivity of the social worker to own knowledge of cultural differences between worker and client
- Professional helping relationship—must be based on mutual respect and trust
- Understanding differing ethnic, culture, class, gender, and age experiences

Community Practice Skills

- Inclusion of diverse groups in community decision making
- Conscientisation—facilitate critical awareness building with community to identify problems and find solutions
- Listen more than talk, learn more than lead
- Community as expert, social worker as facilitator

Source: Burkey, 1993; Hardina, 2003.

problems. Having said this, three important elements must be present before we can expect the community to organize grassroots support around an issue: The community must trust that what they do will make a difference, they must participate in the decisions made about how to proceed, and they must feel empowered in order to mobilize. These three attributes are interrelated, but a discussion of each is in order, along with the skills needed to facilitate them.

BUILDING COMMUNITY TRUST

It is important to understand that as policy practitioners, we will be interacting with people whose experiences diverge largely from our own. Many groups whose experiences have been vital in the formation of American society have been left behind in this country. In order to effectively work in the community to increase community involvement, we must put at the center of our thinking the experiences of groups who have formerly been excluded. Without doing this, other groups are typically judged by the experience of the dominant culture rather than understood on their own terms. By making the experience of previously excluded groups more visible and central to our understanding of the problems we are trying to solve, our perspective shifts, helping us better understand the intersections of race, class, and gender in the experiences of all communities.

According to Anderson and Collins (2001) it is very difficult to understand a community's problems with only partial and distorted knowledge. First, learning about other groups helps you realize the subjective nature of your own perspective. Uehara and associates (1996) suggest that the practitioner must be constantly aware of how her or his own values, beliefs, behaviors, and customs affect the practitioner's understanding of community problems. Therefore, constant introspection and self-reflection on the part of the policy practitioner is critical. Those who experience disenfranchisement have the most potential for analyzing and understanding what those experiences are and how they must be transformed.

Therefore, building trust, particularly in a multicultural environment, requires an effective facilitator who adopts a humble attitude and comes in as a learner as well as a helper. As Gutierrez, Avarez, Nemon, and Lewis (1996) point out, belief and trust in individuals' abilities to develop their own strengths and solutions to problems that they encounter in their communities creates a collective trust that is essential to bring them together. As they come together to discuss the solutions to their problems they will remain united and empowered to carry out the grassroots policy practice efforts. Then it is the policy practitioners' responsibility to facilitate their ef-

DON'T FORGET

Facilitators are there to learn as well as teach; the community understands its own experiences and its own needs.

forts with education on various intervention tactics that need to be performed for the policy to be changed, such as writing letters, using the media, and other strategies that will be discussed in detail in later chapters.

But even as community trust in the process is being developed, the interventions must be participatory and democratic. The policy practitioner must continually remember that in the community arena, she or he is not the expert, but the facilitator.

PARTICIPATION AND DEMOCRATIC DECISION MAKING

Participation focuses on the people who are affected by the problems that policy practitioners are attempting to alleviate. So often, social workers try to advocate for populations without having true participation from the people who are affected. This leads to a situation where, at best, there is little participation by the affected, and at worse, the goals decided upon are not actually in the best interest of the population for whom we advocate. Therefore, participation is defined as the deliberate involvement of the people for whom we advocate in the decision making of the goals and strategies chosen for the policy practice intervention. This means that the focus must be on the persons who are affected by the policies in question or who are experiencing the problem, and they must have opportunities to consider alternatives and choose among them. Participatory practice must be fostered in order to counter the apathy, frustration, and resentment that often arises from feelings of powerlessness to change the policies that affect our lives. To truly advocate for our clients we must become sophisticated in the process of power sharing and foster a sense of sharing, investment in the outcome, and joint responsibility.

Participation can only be achieved through democratic decision making, whereby community members cooperate because they feel ownership over the process. Too often, experts make the decisions for the community and advocate on their behalf. But in policy practice, this results in efforts to make changes without grassroots mobilization. This means that the people power is absent. There are many examples of potentially good policy proposals that have never been passed because decision makers simply did not hear from their constituencies. But without involving the community in the decision-making process, we oftentimes create policies that do not meet the actual needs of the people the policy is designed to assist. The following Putting It Into Practice provides an example of how without grassroots support, legislation will have difficulty being passed, and if it is passed, may not help the population for which it is intended.

The FMLA is a good example of a bill that could have had great potential for assisting families during times of crisis, but the community was never considered when the bill was being proposed. Lobbyists and advocates for families tried to push the bill through. But there was no outcry from the public, no letters of support, no phone calls to legislators. The community did not have a voice in how the bill originated, what the components of the bill would be, or how it could impact them. Little effort was made to educate people on the importance of the legislation. Most community members did not even know that they were not already protected if they or their children became ill and they had to take off work. Furthermore, the policy, as passed, did little to help the poor and working class, because they have a difficult time taking off work without pay. How different this bill might have been had the community been involved in its original intent, and felt ownership regarding its passage.

The suggestions in Rapid Reference 3.2 would ensure that the community is involved in a policy proposal, that they have participated in its origins, and that grassroots support for the policy will be forthcoming. Note that these skill sets are based in community practice principles and are used extensively in community development and community organizing. They can be used, as in our example, to make changes in policies as well.

The use of interpersonal communication, building trust, and using the principles of participation are skill sets that cross the boundaries of communities, agencies, and larger systems levels. Trust is particularly important in all types of policy practice, because conveying integrity is an essential component in policy practice.

Putting It Into Practice

The Case of the Family Medical Leave Act

The Family Medical Leave Act (FMLA) of 1993 is a good example of a policy that floundered without grassroots support and ultimately passed without truly assisting many families who needed it. The FMLA allows employees to take job-protected, unpaid leave for up to 12 weeks in any 12-month period because of a birth of a child, to care for a newborn, a newly adopted or foster child, because the employee is needed to care for a family member (child, spouse, or parent) with a serious health condition, or because the employee's own health condition makes her or him unable to work. An employee who takes FMLA leave is also entitled to keep any employer-provided health benefits that she or he previously had, although she or he must continue to pay any shared health care premium costs while on leave. Under this law the employee also has the right to return to the same position or an equivalent position with equivalent pay, benefits, and working conditions upon return to work.

The FMLA covers all public agencies, including state, local, and federal employers and schools, as well as all private sector employers engaged in commerce or any industry affecting commerce with more than 50 employees who have worked at least 20 or more work weeks. Employees must also have worked at their job for the last 12 months and for at least 1,250 hours within the last year. The employer has a right to 30 days advance notice from the employee if it is practical.

The FMLA is an example of a bill that lost quite a bit of its original intent as a family leave policy, and literally stalled for several years before its passage. It was first introduced in 1985 as the Parental and Disability Act and provided 18 weeks of job-protected leave and offered universal coverage for all employees (Kaitin, 1994). In 1987, the bill was retitled the Family and Medical Leave Act and many compromises were made. The universal component was changed to exempt employers with 50 or less employees and the length of leave was decreased to 12 weeks of coverage. Paid leave was not even introduced in the original bill because advocates did not believe they could find a sponsor for the bill if they required employers to pay employees for their time on leave. Interestingly, the United States was

(continued)

the only industrialized country besides South Africa that did not have a paid family leave law at the time.

Many who would have advocated for the bill pointed out the unpaid component targeted the bill toward the middle class, because poor families would not be able to afford to take the leave. To make matters worse, the coalition of groups trying to get the leave passed had a difficult time gaining grassroots support for the bill. As Kaitin (1994) pointed out in her analysis of the legislative history of the bill, "Constituents tended to be unaware that there were no laws requiring job-protected leave until they were in the midst of a family crisis ... on the other hand, the business community was very resourceful in making its position known to members of Congress through mailings and other grassroots activities" (p. 110). After much lobbying from the top, the bill finally passed in its amended form in 1990, but was vetoed by President Bush. It passed Congress again in 1992, but was again vetoed by President Bush. Finally, in 1993, President Clinton signed the bill into law. Although a weak piece of legislation, the FMLA provides some protection to families who have medical crises and must take time off from work.

≡ Rapid Reference 3.2

. . . .

Suggestions to Facilitate Participation by the Community

• Get to know the community that will be affected by the policy.
• Gain an understanding of the problems faced by the community.
• Reflect with the community on possible solutions to the problems.
• Assist the community in the planning process.
• Build awareness in the community of the plausible actions that may be taken.
• Train the community in grassroots intervention skills.
• Support and encourage community members during the implementation phase.

EMPOWERMENT PRACTICE FOR GRASSROOTS PARTICIPATION

Building trust and encouraging participation is part of the process of empowerment. However, the outcome of empowerment is what will create grassroots participation. The term *empowerment* has become a popular concept, with little understanding of how to actually put it into practice. In social work, we speak of empowerment of clients as an outcome of success. But we must realize that many social workers are not empowered. How can we empower our clients to make changes for themselves if we do not have a sense of empowerment as a profession? Yet the policy practitioner is part of an agency, advocacy organization, or coalition that is advocating for the rights of disenfranchised people. So often, however, the agencies that we are affiliated with are not empowered themselves.

Empowerment is defined as "a construct that links individual strengths and competencies, natural helping systems, and proactive behaviors to matters of social policy and social change" (Zimmerman & Rappaport, 1988, p. 726). Empowerment occurs at the individual, organizational, and community level, with each level impacting the others. Empowerment can be described as a goal, as a process, or as a form of intervention (Gutierrez, GlenMaye, & Delois, 1995). The goal of empowerment practice is to address the lack of power that creates and maintains personal and social ills. Empowerment practice is a method for developing power through self-awareness that supports diversity and individual strengths.

Gutierrez, GlenMaye, and Delois (1995) discuss the process of empowerment practice as a means to the end result of empowerment. The empowerment process is distinguished by its focus on developing critical awareness, increasing feelings of collective self-efficacy, and developing skills for personal, interpersonal, or social change through participation. The outcome of becoming empowered is defined as an increase in the actual power of the client or community so that action can be taken to change and prevent the problems that communities face.

In a review of the empowerment research, Hardina (2003) links em-

DON'T FORGET

Skills needed to create grassroots support:

- Gain community trust.
- Increase democratic participation in decision making.
- Facilitate an increased consciousness of problems and potential solutions.
- Educate on community skills for change.
- Empower, empower, and empower—people, social workers, and organizations.

powerment to improved services in organizations, increased leadership among neighborhood groups, and greater feelings of competency to influence social change. Democratic participation and empowerment cannot be taught. It must be acquired through experience. It is not our role to speak to people about our view of their world or to impose that view on them. As Burkey (1993) points out, you cannot make people self-reliant; people become empowered by their own abilities. People must feel that their own participation and investment leads to positive outcomes for their future. The policy practitioner's job is to understand that it is not helpful to do things for people but to facilitate their ability to do things for themselves. Our job is to give people the tools to make a difference. Effective policy practice requires grassroots support around issues. But the key is that community members must be a part of this process from the beginning, because only they know what they really need. If they are part of the process from the beginning, the likelihood that grassroots participation will occur is much greater.

WORKING WITH COMMUNITY GRASSROOTS ORGANIZATIONS

Community development and grassroots organizing have long been major components of community practice. Both of these two practices can be utilized to organize citizens for political action. Community development is defined by its focus on organizing communities around development plans, preparing citizens to make use of social and economic investments, and using external and internal resources to make those investments (Weil & Gamble, 1995). Community organizing, on the other hand, has traditionally been associated with more social action: organizing communities around a specific issue, mobilizing people around that issue, and utilizing direct action and conflict to win concessions from those in power (Castelloe, Watson, & White, 2002).

According to Fisher (1996) the shift in the national political economy has caused many organizers formally utilizing strategies of social action to become more development minded. He contends that community economic development has become virtually synonymous with neighborhood organizing since the 1980s. In his historical analysis, he states that in the 1960s and the first part of the 1970s, when the political activist type of neighborhood organizing came to dominate, the national political economy both supported the change and was the product of it. It was the grassroots resistance of the southern civil rights movement, the student New Left, and the rebellion in black urban slums that pushed the national political economy left. These movements then expanded the political discourse to legitimate grassroots resistance, and ultimately social policy, to address the needs of the poor and people of color.

Beginning around 1980, however, organizing found government support drastically cut. Concern with broader social issues and social action receded. In the economic crisis of the past few decades, economic survival became the paramount issue for most individuals, organizations, businesses, and cities. Fisher contends that as economic support for social services and solving social problems declined and as political discourse in the nation revolved around free market solutions to all problems, neighborhood organizing efforts moved into the business of economic development. Most political activist neighborhood organizing efforts during the 1980s and early 1990s adopted more moderate strategies, and a more moderated version of oppositional politics. I do not believe that this has greatly shifted in the new millennium.

Community economic development and building community partnerships with business and local government became the dominant form of neighborhood organizing because of the demands and constraints of organizing in a neoconservative political economy. Given the dramatic tensions and shifts occurring worldwide, both in the global economy and nationally, we are likely to see continued focus on community economic development as global competition increases and the government's focus on domestic social needs continues to wane. Fisher (1996) states that although community development does not make the kinds of social changes that organizing does, it helps build the capacity for governance, gets advocates to the bargaining table, and makes incremental changes.

Castelloe, Watson, and White (2002) take the strong points of development, organizing, and education and integrate them in their practice, which they call "participatory change" (p. 7). They say the major strengths of participatory development are that it facilitates participation and emphasizes the capacity of grassroots groups, but its major limitation is that development rarely is used to analyze or question the social forces that result in oppression. The major strengths of each of these community practice models are their organizing capabilities. Each provides an avenue for bringing communities together in a natural alliance that can be used for policy change.

In the planning process, it is very important to find out if there are already organizations working on identified problems in the community, as well as to find out who may want to partner in working on those issues. Grassroots organizations should be used as a resource to identify interests and utilize existing groups who may already be mobilized around similar political issues. First, already existing community-based organizations, such as those described previously, have a membership base that is generally highly active. Second, there is no need to duplicate efforts. If your task force can find other organizations that are already active in some ways, you can pool resources, split up tasks, or develop your own tasks that will complement what they are already doing. Although tips on developing community organizations are beyond the scope of this book, Rapid Reference 3.3 provides handbooks for practitioners who desire to gain skills in developing grassroots organizations.

≡ *Rapid Reference 3.3*

Handbooks for Developing Community Organizations

Bobo, K., Kendall, J., & Max, S. (1996). *Organizing for social change: A manual for activists in the 1990s* (2nd ed.). Santa Ana, CA: Seven Locks Press.

Kahn, S. (1994). *How people get power.* Washington, DC: NASW Press.

Nadeau, D. (1996). *Counting our victories: Popular education and organizing.* New Westminster, British Columbia, Canada: Repeal the Deal Productions.

Pick, M. (1993). *How to save your neighborhood, city, or town.* San Francisco: Sierra Club Books.

SUMMARY

Basic social work skills of facilitation, relationship building, communication, and participation are essential in all aspects of the policy practice process. Particularly important are the skills in building grassroots support, because changes in policymaking at all levels is much more likely to be effective if there is community support. Having the skills to work with already-established community groups is a good way to increase support because these groups already have active memberships. As will be seen in upcoming chapters, good interpersonal skills will be required again and again as we build our repertoire of skills and strategies to work in multiple-target systems for change.

🔸 TEST YOURSELF 🔸

Suppose that a housing project in your area is slated to be closed and demolished. There are 200 residents in the project and no clear plan as to where they will go. You work at a local homeless shelter and you are afraid the homeless population of families is about to skyrocket.

1. What skills can be used to approach the population of the housing project?

(continued)

2. What skills would you use with public officials to address the problems that your agency foresees?

3. What should you take into consideration before approaching either of these groups?

4. List three individual interpersonal communication skills that all social workers should possess that would be appropriate to use in this case.

5. List three community practice skills that would be helpful in mobilizing the housing residents.

6. What issues must a social worker understand in order to effectively build a community's trust?

7. Discuss why the participation of the housing tenants is essential to a successful policy practice effort.

8. Describe how the failure of the FMLA provides examples of how to avoid similar failures in our work with the housing project.

9. Why should an empowerment approach be utilized in trying to help the tenants of the housing project?

10. Discuss any benefits to seeking out other grassroots organizations in the community to assist in your efforts.

Four

COMMUNICATING WITH THE PUBLIC THROUGH THE MEDIA

Effective use of the media is an important skill that can be used in a variety of policy practice strategies and cuts across issues related to organizations, community problems, local and state government, and so on. There are numerous reasons why policy practitioners may want to use the media. It may be as simple as advertising an upcoming fundraising event. Or there may be a social problem that needs public attention. Or we may want to put pressure on elected officials or bureaucratic organizations to make changes to policy. Regardless of the goals and objectives of the policy practice plan, the media can and should be used as needed. However, as with any strategy, it should be used cautiously and with ample thought as to how it relates to the overriding goal of the chosen intervention, as well as the potential unintended consequences that can occur through its use.

While this chapter focuses on communicating with the public, it is largely through the media that this occurs. Using the media allows us to get out the most information to the largest number of people. But there is a method to media madness. There are certain times when one type of media outlet is better than another, and thought must go into deciding which media outlet is the best venue for a given issue.

USE OF THE MEDIA IN POLICY PRACTICE

The ability to use the media to relay information, discuss issues, and report upcoming events is an invaluable skill for social workers to have. It is important to understand which media outlet is most appropriate for our goals and objectives, as well as to understand which choice of media gives us the greatest advantage to get our message across. For example, there are certain circumstances when it will be best to write a press release or a letter to the editor, because the writer has more control over her or his written word. In other situations, one will have a greater likelihood of getting press attention by inviting a reporter to an event or scheduling an interview. But beware, because depending on the format one chooses, the social worker will have more or less autonomy over what is written. As will be seen as we go through each type of media venue, control over the written word is very important. The following uses of the media are first described and then discussed in terms of the control that the policy practitioner has in how the information is disseminated.

Op-Eds and Letters to the Editor

Op-eds (also known as opinion editorials or commentaries), provide much autonomy to the author. However, op-eds are also generally invited, or if they may be submitted, there are few that are selected. Although they are more difficult to get published than a letter to the editor, they can be longer and provide opportunities to discuss in-depth issues and current problems, both locally and nationally. The following are some helpful hints on how to get op-eds published:

- Find out the name of the op-ed page editor. Find out the policy for acceptance, the length specifications, and the address and fax numbers. Not all newspapers will accept unsolicited materials, but most do.
- Establish yourself as an expert on your topic or as representing a larger organization. After a few submissions, editors will begin to recognize your name and become interested.
- Editors receive about thirty op-eds per day in larger cities; if it is poorly written or needs too much editing, they will throw it out without reading it.
- Don't exceed your word limit: write concisely.

Other tips on op-eds, given by Stoesz (1993), include: (a) Use a catchy title and write the op-ed in a punchy style, without footnotes. (b) Numerical data are useful. Use them in a limited way to illustrate important points. A well-chosen anecdote may be more powerful than a long string of statistics. (c) The op-ed should close with solutions: How might the community proceed from here? How can we resolve the problem? (d) A brief biography of the author should appear at the bottom. Although newspapers generally pay for an op-ed, many smaller papers do not.

A good letter to the editor may be a better alternative, since it is easier to get published. In fact, more people read the letters to the editor than the op-eds. These are generally much shorter than an op-ed or commentary, 100 to 300 words in length, depending on the paper. Lively debates can begin with letters to the editor and run for several weeks. Several years ago, I wrote a letter to an editor during a debate about raising taxes to fund our Medicaid Managed Care program. It was a very politically charged issue at the time, with writers accusing those who supported the tax increase of wanting a socialist government. The letter that I wrote was in response to a previous letter decrying our attempt to provide health care to the poor as undemocratic. In it, I compared social programs in other industrialized countries to the United States in how they could provide health care and other programs for all of their citizens. I also took the opportunity to discuss the politically charged "socialist" debate. The following Putting It Into Practice provides a copy of the letter. For several weeks people wrote in to comment on that letter, both positively and negatively (one person called me a lava lamp liberal!) Then others would write in to further the exchange. It was certainly a way to bring an issue out for public debate and keep it in the public eye over an extended period of time.

A couple of issues should be noted about the letter. It went over the word limit. Some editors will publish a letter that goes over the word limit if they find it particularly interesting. Apparently the editor liked this one (perhaps because it was a bit provocative), because he or she also gave it a title and a cartoon, which is done for just a few of the letters sent in. Also, note that a previous letter to the editor was cited in my letter. This is

Putting It Into Practice

Letters to the Editor

Taxes Could Fund Health Insurance

Editor, The News-Sentinel:

I read with interest the letters to the editor regarding the various sides of the tax cut issue (Aug. 10). I write this letter in hopes of adding clarity and information to the debate.

It is unsettling to me to think that people may equate increased social benefits from the government with socialist countries such as Cuba and the Soviet Union, which are not democratic. The issue is not quite so black and white.

There are many democratic nations that have a nice mix between capitalism and socialism and still maintain democracy. Democracy is a philosophical ideal, while capitalism and socialism are economic systems. There are many countries that have balanced out socialized policies with capitalism—most of Europe, in fact.

U.S. citizens should be aware that, out of all the industrial nations (except South Africa), the United States alone has no guaranteed health insurance for its citizens. This is particularly sad given that it is the lowest-paid workers who suffer the burden of a lack of health insurance, not our poorest citizens who have Medicaid (or TennCare) to fall back on.

Other social programs that higher taxes have paid for in European countries are children's allowances and free college educations. We don't want to pay higher taxes, yet those of us without parents who can afford to help with our educations end up with $30,000 to $50,000 in school debt to pay back for the rest of our lives. Some incentive to get an education.

And what kind of capitalism is this anyway, where the largest corporations have turned into such monopolies that the little guy (our old mom and pop businesses) can't even compete in the market anymore? And if you have a small business, health insurance is so high it's unaffordable.

No, I think we are looking far too simplistically at these issues. It's not a choice between extreme capitalism and socialism.

Other countries have found ways to care for their citizens in a civilized way and still maintain both democracy and capitalism.

The argument that we don't want to pay more taxes for increased social benefits does not take into consideration the extra money we end up paying out of our pockets for health care, college educations and the social costs from 36 million people who remain in poverty, many of whom work.

In a country where the poverty line is higher than the minimum wage, we'd better start thinking about increased security and benefits for our workers, even if it means higher taxes, but a more civilized society offering greater opportunity in the long run.

Cynthia Rocha

Knoxville

Reprinted with permission of the *Knoxville News Sentinel.*

important because the letters should be in response to something that is currently an issue in the community, state, or nation.

In summary, the op-ed and letters to the editor are very good ways to get a message out about a local problem, use as part of a community awareness campaign, or to suggest an alternative policy. They also offer a great amount of control over what is printed. Rarely do editors change the content of a letter or op-ed, so the writer has control over her or his message. Finally, except for the front page and the comics, the letters to the editor are the most widely read part of a newspaper.

Using letters to the editor as part of a community change project is sometimes ideal, because, as previously mentioned, the issue can be kept in the forefront of the public's mind for quite some time, depending on how many people write in to respond. In the example given earlier, the subject stayed in the paper for about 6 weeks, as one person wrote in to negatively reflect on the idea of national health care, prompting another person to respond in favor, and so on.

In a policy practice project focusing on a local wheel tax issue, a student task force decided to make sure that the issue stayed at the forefront by strategically writing letters each week to respond to previously written letters by their own task force members. Use this strategy with caution, however. If the editor believes it is a group effort, he or she will not publish the letters, and it could affect future letter publication as well. But it is a good strategy if done carefully and correctly. Rapid Reference 4.1 provides tips on how to make sure your letter has a good chance of being selected.

News Releases

News releases are another way to obtain media coverage and also have quite a bit of control over what is printed. News releases are used to announce an event, a new program, or a new service. They are written very much like a newspaper article and *if* they are reprinted without many changes to the original copy, it is hard to distinguish them from a short

≡ Rapid Reference 4.1

A Few Tips on Writing Letters to the Editor

- Check with the paper to see what the accepted length of the letter should be.
- Try to connect the letter to an article or letter previously published.
- Edit your letter very carefully. A letter with typos and grammatical errors will go straight to the trash.
- Never attack an opponent—it may be good reading, but very bad form. Good policy practitioners don't burn bridges.
- Make your most important points first and last.
- If you want to use statistics, use them sparingly; most people prefer a good story.
- Try to offer a solution to the problem.
- Make sure you sign your letter and provide a telephone number.

article. Notice the *if.* Some papers may bury them with another release or shorten the prose considerably. It depends largely on what is in the news on the day of release. If it is a slow news day, the likelihood that the news release will run in its entirety is greater. Brody (1985) offers the following checklist on creating a news release:

- Type the release on 8½ × 11 inch paper, double spaced, with wide margins so the editor has room to write on it.
- Identify your organization in the upper left corner of the page and provide the name of a contact person and telephone number.
- Include release instructions, typed in all capital letters, such as FOR IMMEDIATE RELEASE, or include a date. Do not delay the release date by more than a few days so it doesn't get lost on someone's desk.
- About one-third from the top of the page, put the heading of the release, centered and typed in all capital letters.
- Write the release like a news story, answering the questions who, what, when, where, why, and how.
- Include the most important information in the lead paragraph and the remaining information in descending order of importance.
- Use quotes to liven up the prose and make your points strongly. Be sure your facts, figures, and quotes are absolutely correct.
- Use active verbs, check your spelling and grammar.
- Keep the release brief and factual, with short sentences and paragraphs. Try not to let the release run longer than a page. If it runs past the first page, type "MORE" in parenthesis at the bottom of the page. At the top of the next page type "2 of 2" or "Page 2."
- At the end of the release, type "-30-" or "###" to indicate it is finished (pp. 84–85).

The following Putting It Into Practice provides an example of a news release. This particular release was printed in its entirety with very little

Putting It Into Practice

Name of Organization
Contact Person:
Phone number
FOR RELEASE: Date

ACTING OUT: TEENS PORTRAY CONFLICT THROUGH THE ARTS

They may not be Broadway bound yet but some teens are helping to educate their peers and the community through the "Teen Acting Troupe." They perform dramatic roles on difficult topics, including family violence, sexual assault, and nonviolent conflict resolution. Public performances are scheduled for 7 P.M. on August 17 and 24 at the Downtown theatre.

"I don't want what happened to me to happen to anyone else," one troupe member said. "That's why when I heard about the Acting Troupe I had to join." The troupe is made up of fifteen teens, from all walks of life. The teens meet weekly in a program designed to help them find healthy ways to address violence in their lives. "We felt that the program could help teens explore nonviolent ways to solve conflicts and educate the community at the same time," says Jane Doe, coordinator of the program.

Doe says the program has a three-fold purpose. Teens explore the violence they face in their lives with peers who are in similar situations, use drama to increase the community's awareness of violence teens must endure, and practice skills to address the violence some face on a daily basis. "I can't say I'll never argue again," one Teen Troupe member said, "but I know I can try other things if someone resorts to violence."

###

editing. However, if it is a busy news day, it may get couched into an obscure section of the newspaper, or even added onto another release that is of similar content. Therefore, although the writer has control over what is written, where it is placed is often out of the writer's control.

Public Service Announcements

Public Service Announcements (PSAs) are also a good way to get messages to the public. They are used for several purposes, but generally it is to bring attention to an issue or problem in the community and potential solutions to the problem. PSAs are generally not accepted that focus on a specific political point of view, however. We have all seen PSAs since we were kids. They look very much like an advertisement, but they are focused on a public issue. For example, baby boomers like myself may remember Smokey the Bear—"Only YOU can prevent forest fires." I always thought that was some kind of commercial, but now I realize it was a public service announcement. Another favorite of mine was the PSA that used an egg and fried it in a pan, "This is your brain—this is your brain on drugs." Some of the more current examples focus on the war on drugs and smoking cigarettes. The reader probably is familiar with a relatively new set of PSAs called "Parents: The Anti-Drug." One example is the parent who has a short conversation with his or her child about not doing drugs and then says "we have a lot of time to talk about this." The camera turns to the child, who is still in a high chair. Another is a parent talking to a teenager about not smoking. The teen does not appear to be interested, but the next frame flashes to a picture of someone offering a cigarette and the teen says "no thanks." These are short, powerful messages that make one point in a few seconds.

PSAs are usually prerecorded and sent to radio or television stations. They are utilized extensively by nonprofit agencies. It is a free message to the public and the station has a certain number reserved for its contribution to the community. PSAs are generally only 15 to 30 seconds long, so great care has to be taken to deliver the message with the most impact in the shortest amount of time.

Although you may want to tape your message and send it to the station, some stations will bring you into the studio and use their own equipment to videotape your announcement. Contact various television and radio stations to find out what their policies are. A student task force at the University of Tennessee used the resources of one television station to videotape a PSA on gangs and violence with a group of teenagers. They taped it in the station for the task force and aired that PSA for over 8 months.

There are a few important tips about PSAs. First, make sure that you pay attention to the audience you want to target. In the previous example, the task force made sure that the teenagers chosen were everyday kids. They did not look like models or actors. They were diverse, boys and girls, thick and thin, racially mixed. The task force attempted to pick kids that others could relate to. Second, make sure that the message is clear and makes one important point. Don't try to put too much into one message. Fifteen seconds goes by in a flash, so the message must be concise and to the point.

A few tips on the mechanics of a PSA are included in Rapid Reference 4.2.

Community Calendars

Community calendars, also called community bulletin boards, are another way to get a free message out to the public through newspapers, television, and radio stations. Community announcements should be short, with only the event, time, place, and contact information included. Newspapers generally have a section where community events are located. The local radio stations will make occasional announcements of events

≡ Rapid Reference 4.2

Tips on Public Service Announcements (PSAs)

- Call your radio or television stations and speak to the public service director to assess the willingness to produce and/or accept a PSA.
- Use your interpersonal skills to create a good relationship with the station personnel.
- Submit a potential idea or script to the station for approval.
- A 30-second PSA is only about 80 words. Make two—a 30-second and a 15-second PSA. It has a better chance of being accepted.
- Your organization's name should appear at the end of the PSA.
- After your initial phone call, follow up. Producers are busy.

that are coming up. Television stations generally air community calendars late at night or early in the morning, or they may read off lists of upcoming community events during their news broadcasts. Community television gives quite a bit of air space to community listings, sometimes giving entire time slots to community events, scrolling each one slowly.

Interviews and News Coverage

Interviews and news coverage are other tactics that can be used to get a message out to the public. Interviews can be obtained in a number of ways. Sometimes it is simply a newsworthy event, such as an award that is being given at your agency, or a press conference that has been called. Get to know the reporters who cover stories in your area of interest. Oftentimes social workers are able to identify themselves as an expert in a certain area. Because reporters are always looking for different perspectives when writing a story, they will remember you and may contact you for an interview. But remember to be cautious with your words. Oftentimes interviews offer very little control over what is being printed. Choose your words carefully. If it is a newspaper report, provide only information that you want to be printed. If it is a television interview, remember that producers are looking for sound bites. So make it simple and to the point. It is often difficult to do this, because issues are usually complex. Think about how you can get your main point across as simply and directly as possible. Run it by colleagues to see if it comes across the way you wish. By maintaining good relationships with reporters, you will generally be allowed to review an interview for accuracy before it is published. I have seen many an interview, however, with inaccurate information, so try to be clear and choose your words as carefully and as simply as possible.

Interviews may also be appropriate on radio and television. Many local news channels carry human interest stories, and it is appropriate to contact them to assess their interest in your issue or upcoming event. Most local stations have news shows that are not just the evening news, but are aired a half hour to an hour earlier and have news highlights, interviews, and public interest stories. Watch the shows for a few weeks to understand the types of human interest stories each channel produces. Then contact the producer of the show to see if they are interested in doing a spot about your organization, fund-raiser, or an issue that your group is working on. I have seen fund-raisers publicized, new programs introduced, and varying groups proposing solutions to community problems addressed on these programs.

Public television is another option for interviews. They often have call-in shows where groups can discuss issues, upcoming political campaigns, and a number of other items of interest. According to the Michigan Public Policy Institute (2001), 50 percent of all cable subscribers watch their community public access channels on a regular basis. As with the news shows, watch your public access channel for a few weeks to find out which shows might be appropriate for an interview, then call to talk with the producer to see if your interests match their focus. If your group decides to do a call-in show, make sure that you have people lined up to call in with questions that will allow you to make important points that you want to make sure are addressed.

Radio talk shows, very popular right now, have guest speakers on a number of issues. Check and make sure that your topic is appropriate for the show first, however. Unless you are willing to be thrown into the fire, make sure that the host does not have a particular stance beforehand that is in direct opposition to yours. News is news, and some shows, particularly on talk radio, are interested in controversy. Just as we should check what topics televised shows typically cover, we also need to check out different radio talk shows. Some of them are really interested in different points of views, especially if you are perceived as an expert in a particular area.

Given the lack of control that one may have in an interview, a few tips are in order. First, before you go on a show (particularly on the radio) have your main points you want to make firmly in your mind. Repeat these over and over. If you feel you are being baited by your host, stay poised, calm, and continue to repeat your message. Another situation that could likely occur is that after you receive news coverage from another

event, particularly if it was controversial, you may be deluged
with calls from reporters and talk
show hosts asking for comments.
From my experience, it's best to
have some responses prepared for
them. In particular, if it is a poten-

> ## DON'T FORGET
>
> Choose your words carefully in in-
> terviews. Repeat your main point
> over and over. Stay calm. Choose
> a few good sound bites.

tially hostile conversation on the part of the interviewer, it is still best to
speak with them for a moment. Making a "no comment" or telling the station you don't have time to make a statement on the show is an invitation
for the host and callers to denigrate your position without any defense on
your part. Continue to use your interpersonal skills—be friendly, be firm,
stick to your original position, and try to not get flustered by unflattering
comments. The point here is not to scare people away from interviews that
might be controversial; these must be addressed. The point is to be prepared, and know that people may disagree with you and attempt to catch
you off guard. Don't let them.

News Coverage

News coverage is a bit different from an interview. Although reporters
may ask for an interview while covering an event, they may also simply
cover it and take the liberty of reporting the event from whatever perspective they choose. Typical news coverage has the least amount of control
of what is reported. News coverage can be obtained in a number of ways.
Forums, public meetings, and various events can be held. Well-known
speakers can be invited, awards given to public officials, or public fund-
raisers can all be used for media coverage. The important thing is that the
news outlets must be contacted prior to the event. It is not enough to write
a press release; a phone call to the news desk or a friendly reporter is in
order. It is also important to mention that specific reporters are generally
assigned to specific types of news. For example, the same reporter covered both a protest by students at the university for lack of handicapped

accessibility and a story about a middle school student who was suspended for wearing sagging pants. That reporter covered everything that had to do with education. When calling for news coverage, if the event is photo friendly (a good picture is worth a thousand words) don't forget to suggest bringing along a photographer; the newspaper will not always automatically send a photographer.

Action Methods

One sure way to obtain news coverage is with some form of action. Although these kinds of tactics are more confrontational, they are also very likely to make the news. Coercive strategies should be used with caution, and generally only when cooperation and negotiation with a target system have not been met with the desired response or have not received enough attention. Coercive messages may be effective when no other recourse exists and when decision makers feel vulnerable to adverse publicity or to coercion. But coercive messages also carry risks. As Jansson (2003) points out, if decision makers do not feel vulnerable to coercion, they may harden their positions and take retaliatory measures.

Coercive strategies involve social action techniques to attract media attention when there is resistance to change. In order to force a response it may be important to disrupt business as usual, show strength in numbers, and keep the momentum going with continuous pressure. Such strategies include calling a press conference, teach-ins, protest marches, and other activities to get the public's attention toward an important issue. These strategies are designed to get the attention of decision makers and the public. A well-strategized plan is needed to ensure press coverage. Using these media tips and maintaining good relationships with reporters is essential to making action strategies work.

Here are a couple of action strategy examples that have worked in the past to get news attention. A local grassroots organization wanted to bring attention to problems with the state's Medicaid managed care program. They used research that had just been completed on the problems with the managed care system to call a press conference on the issue. They then put out the word to their members, through e-mails and phone calls, that there would be a press conference to release the results of the study. They organized volunteers to attend the press conference. Shortly before the press arrived, protestors emerged in bandages, wheelchairs, and carrying signs alluding to the problems they were having receiving care. When the press arrived it was quite a spectacle. This is an important point because television crews, in particular, may only stay for a few minutes, so everything must be in place beforehand. Then the speaker began to give a brief summary of the findings. It was a well-organized affair. The research report gave legitimacy to their cause, while the protestors created an interesting news event.

A second example that was interesting was a honk-in that occurred at the state capitol during a debate in the general assembly to raise state taxes. This was actually organized by a radio talk show host, who beckoned people who did not want their taxes raised to drive to the capitol and let their voices be heard through their horns. Hundreds of cars blocked the downtown area with signs hanging out of their windows that read "NO NEW TAXES," honking their horns and blocking traffic. This went on for the entire day, as some cars left and others arrived. Needless to say, it was quite controversial, but it also received a lot of news coverage.

Create a Media File

Different events require different types of media use. For example, if your organization is having a fundraiser, you probably want to write a press release, or get listed on a community calendar, rather than call a press conference. It is a good idea to create a media file. A media file divides up the various news venues and contacts by each media type. For example, one section is for community calendars. All of the radio stations, newspapers, and televisions have community calendar sections and contact people. For each one, write the name of the station or newspaper, who the contact is, the fax numbers and telephone numbers, and how far in advance they

DON'T FORGET

Create a media file where you have easy access to editors and contact people for various news outlets.

want to have the information. Do another section for public service announcements, and for radio and television talk and call-in shows. For community calendars, in particular, it is suggested that a follow-up phone call be made to ensure they have received your fax or e-mail and also to discuss when you may expect it to be published.

For letters to the editors, op-eds, and news releases, write down the number of words allowed, who the editor is for that section, their contact information, and any other pertinent information that has been accumulated in previous contacts with them. Do the same thing for news events, who the reporters are that cover various subject matter, and so on. Even in a small metropolitan area, the number of contacts that will go into the media file is surprising. Update it periodically, as people, phone numbers, and even time lines may change.

SUMMARY

There are many ways to get messages out to the general public, and the media is the primary venue. But it must be used deliberately, with thought given beforehand to which venue best suits the message that one wants to send. Think about who needs to see the message and how the message will be received. Keep the target system in mind, and always make sure that the tactic chosen is in line with the goals of the policy practice intervention.

It is very important to base part of your decision on how to publicize your information with the knowledge of how much control one wishes to maintain over what is being reported. This is especially important to consider if the information one wishes to convey is sensitive or potentially controversial. To sum up, news releases and letters to the editor keep the most control in the hands of the policy practitioner and are the most likely to get published. Op-eds and public service announcements also allow control over what is written, but are less likely to be published. Interviews and general news coverage offer the least amount of control over what is published and are subject to the interpretation of the reporter.

⚓ TEST YOURSELF ⚓

Look at the following objectives that were chosen for a policy practice plan. Discuss which type of media coverage would be best suited for each.

1. To create public awareness about an increase in sexual assault on a college campus.

2. To provide information about an upcoming workshop on family violence.

3. To publicize a new program to help teen parents obtain a high school diploma.

4. To put pressure on public officials to pass a law requiring motorcyclists to wear helmets.

5. To create public discourse on the plight of the working poor.

6. To try to pressure the city and/or state by bringing awareness to a toxic waste dump in your community.

7. To try to increase community involvement in saving an historic building.

8. To publicize a program to assist the uninsured to obtain medication.

9. To gain support for a piece of legislation pending in Congress.

10. To attract community members who are interested in joining your Coalition to End Hunger.

Five

UTILIZING TECHNOLOGY IN POLICY PRACTICE

Technology has changed the face of policy practice in recent years. The ease with which we can now use the computer to create professional brochures, fliers, business cards, and newsletters can save money and time for groups and organizations that work on policy issues. Even more phenomenal is the pace at which the Internet is being used. Between 2000 and 2005, for example, Internet use among Americans went from 46 percent to 67 percent of the population who go online (Pew Charitable Trust, 2006). The use of cell phones is another technological advancement that is growing and advancing at a rapid pace. Just 10 years ago cell phones were big and bulky, expensive, and used by few in the United States. Now cell phones are small, inexpensive, digital, and can be used to text message, e-mail, and access the Internet.

This chapter will explore the pros and cons in the use of technology in policy practice and give some practical skills in using technology to advocate and organize people to participate in the policy process. We must be aware that not everyone has access to technology, and therefore our target population and the populations that we may want to partner with for policy change must be considered carefully before we embark on an exciting trip through cyberspace. But even if we find that some forms of technology will not be effective in our planning stage, there is always room for innovative and creative ways to use technology. It is simply very important to analyze where the use of technology is important, and where it may or may not have the desired outcome. These issues, along with tips on how to become more technologically savvy, will be explored in this chapter.

DESKTOP PUBLISHING

Most major word processing computer programs, such as Microsoft Word and WordPerfect, now have the ability to do desktop publishing. Newsletters, brochures, business cards, and other published materials can be made at home or in your office. Most programs have templates, or *wizards,* that tell you exactly how to create the material and what usually goes where.

Brochures and Fact Sheets

Brochures and fact sheets are fast and easy ways to get a message out to the public, agencies, public officials, and others. They are easy to make and look very professional. Brochures can be used to provide information about a variety of topics; they are made in such a way that there is optimal space provided to give information, and they can be mailed by simply folding them and stapling one end. The student groups at the University of Tennessee have used brochures for a variety of purposes. They have distributed brochures to school administrators and students to create awareness of the lack of handicapped access on campus and to elderly clients to provide information on how to use free drug programs. Small organizations give clients brochures that elaborate on the services they provide. The list goes on and on. The following Putting It Into Practice provides tips on where to put information in a brochure. Most word processing programs also provide templates for ease of creating brochures, as well as many other publishing materials, and some other suggestions on where to put certain information.

Don't try to fill the panels entirely with text. White (empty) spaces make the brochure more inviting and easier to read. Graphics can be added to the panel by going to the insert menu and selecting clip art to insert. Brochure panels are usually read in the order listed. While the sixth panel is the cover and gets looked at first, most people actually begin reading on the first panel, which is on the inside cover. Therefore, panels 4, 5, and 6 are the outside of the brochure and 1, 2, and 3 are the inside of the bro-

Putting It Into Practice

Brochure Panels

Panel 4	Panel 5	Panel 6
People who contributed to the activity.	If you plan to mail out your brochure, this panel will be where the address and stamp are placed. The word processing program will automatically put the return address sideways.	**Brochure Title** (clip art is nice here) Name of Organization
Panel 1	**Panel 2**	**Panel 3**
Who we are	What we do	Action
Features (the description of your product, service or organization)	Benefits (the description of its benefits to your audience or clients)	Action (what you want people to do after reading the brochure)

chure. When the brochure is printed out there will be two pages, panels 4, 5, 6 on one page and panels 1, 2, 3 on the next. These should be copied back to back. Since panel 6 will be read first, use a picture or clip art, as it livens up the brochure and makes the reader more interested in reading on. If it is about a local event, don't forget to list the sponsors on panel 4.

Newsletters

The primary goal of a newsletter is to keep an organization's membership informed about issues affecting the group. The newsletter should reserve the first article as a cover article that gives a current update on a policy or problem that is being addressed by the members. There should also be an article regarding upcoming events and who to contact for more information. Membership forms or donation forms can appear at the bottom of the newsletter so that members and others can cut them out and return them.

Depending on what issue you are working on, a secondary purpose of the newsletter is to inform community members, other organizations, politicians, or the press of your activities. This strategy should be done with some thought. Who do you want to target besides your membership? Since some articles in the newsletter may be targeting specific state agencies, school boards, legislators, and to alert members of an upcoming action, this may not be the time to share your newsletter with just anyone. But at other times—when you are writing about accomplishments, for example—you would want to send a copy to pertinent officials or to the media.

Most word processing programs will have one or two newsletter formats to choose from. Choose a format that is easy to read. The following Putting It Into Practice gives an example of a newsletter that was produced with a template from a simple word processing program. High school students at a small, community-based nonprofit school designed a professional-looking newsletter. Note the liberal use of clip art and boxes to bring out particular requests or to highlight certain areas of the newsletter. Also note that changing the font for different sections can liven up the newsletter as well as draw attention to particular issues. Just as a side note, because the students had covered all of the articles they wanted to, and there was still a little bit of space on the second page, the dove on the back became a lot larger!

The following check list describes the pull-down menus to find templates in both Microsoft Word and WordPerfect:

✓ Microsoft Word 2003: Go to File/New and select Templates (for earlier versions of Word, select Wizards. Depending on the version of Microsoft Word that you are using, some of the

Laurel High School

Volume 1 Issue 1   February 1999

Students Tackle Important Issues

By Joel Marshall

Laurel High School's Student Council was formed last year by students concerned with issues and problems facing the school. Some of the issues being dealt with so far are scheduling conflicts, student credit deficiencies, student admission, and drug issues. The council met several times over the summer to work on changes in this year's scheduling of classes. The council has no formal membership, but is composed of students willing to convene whenever necessary to take responsibility for the well being of the school. We feel that the student council is a wonderful step towards making Laurel an even more tightly knit community. ❦

Family Night '98

By Charlotte Maxwell-Jones

On the eve of Oct. 29, 1998 the Laurel students and faculty hosted a presentation of some of their school-related projects and activities. Judd Hoek showed sculptures made from twisted wire and other 'found' objects. Misha Ramsey displayed hand-sewn dolls based on her favorite manga (Japanese comic book) characters. The Conversational Spanish class sang "La Bamba", accompanied by Fletcher Stewart and Harold Haffner on guitar. The video making class presented some of their recent works. Ben Jefferson displayed his talent as a weaponsmith. With these and other displays of talent and plenty of good food, Family Night was deemed a great success by all involved. ❖

✂ (cut out)

If you would like to make a donation, please provide your name and address. Be sure to indicate what program you would prefer to support! Mailing address: LHS 1539 Laurel Avenue, Knoxville, TN 37916

☐ Travel Club $_____   ☐ Rock Climbing Team $_____
☐ Arts Program $_____   ☐ Computer Lab
☐ Other: $_____   ☐ No Preference
TOTAL: $_____

Please make all checks payable to Laurel High School. All donations are tax-deductible!

Your Name: _____
Your Address: _____
Street _____ Apt. # _____ City _____ State _____ Zip _____

LHS Climbing Team Hits the Top

(But Not Hard Enough to Leave a Bruise)

By Kelly Brown
Climbing Team Coach

This year the ten members of the LHS climbing team are again competing against many area high schools. Last year Laurel came in second place citywide. This year we are contenders for the crown. The team has gained a good deal of respect (and fear) from many of the area teams. The support from the student body, staff, and parents has been tremendous. Please call the school (525-3885) if you would like a schedule. 🖼

If you would like to visit the school as a guest speaker, please call 525-3885 and ask for Claudia!

2

Travel Opportunities
Diversity Through Music

By Joel Marshall and Charlotte Maxwell-Jones

Four students from Laurel High School raised funds for a 3-week field trip to the United Kingdom with chaperone and facilitator Peggy Hall. Traveling through England, Scotland and Wales, they visited historical landmarks, observed the surrounding cultures, and adapted to their companions' diverse traveling styles. The expedition was an overall success, and LHS will continue to have these programs available to industrious students. ➤

✂ (cut out)

Laurel High School Newsletter

By Claudia White
Principal, LHS

Clean Teen is a support group designed to promote healthy choices for youth in the Knoxville community rather than alcohol and drug use. The program is designed to have formal support group meetings and physical activities that interest the group. It is open to any teenager who has the intention and desire to stay clean from drugs and alcohol. Currently, our group participates in rock climbing, paleo-anthropological activities and massage therapy. ☺

More Travel Opportunities
Spanish Trip

By Cynthia Rocha

The Conversational Spanish class is planning a road trip to Mexico on March 15, 1999. We will go through San Antonio and visit the Alamo and the Missions. We will then travel to Nuevo Laredo, Mexico, shop at the mercados, walk through the zocalos, and visit the museums. Although we have done some fundraising, we are still raising money. If you would like to donate for the trip, we would appreciate it. Or come by our yard sale this Saturday and Sunday, march 6th & 7th at Laurel!

Thanks!

We are trying to build a database of LHS student, faculty, and alumni addresses and phone numbers! Please fill out the form below and mail to Claudia White. We would like to have mailing/ e-mail addresses and phone numbers on file for as many of us as possible. Thank you for your cooperation!

Name: _____
Address: _____ Apt. # _____
City: _____ State: _____ ZIP: _____
Home Phone: (___) _____ E-Mail: _____

templates (brochures, for example) will be on the computer and others can be obtained by going online.

✓ WordPerfect 11: Go to File/New/Start New Project; under the "Create New" tab there is a pull-down menu with twenty or so options. Choose "Creative Projects" for brochures, certificates, newsletters, and greeting cards. Choose "Publish" for business cards.

Other Desktop Publishing Ideas

It's easy to be creative with desktop publishing. Fliers are fun to create to inform people about upcoming events, and pictures for fliers can be downloaded, either from your own jpeg files or from clip art that comes with most programs. Word processing programs are so advanced that professional fliers can be made that look as if you just paid a printing company to print them for you. Templates for business cards are also included in both Microsoft Word and WordPerfect.

Aside from these ideas, which have templates included in the program, there are a lot of creative ways to utilize simple programs. For example, the following Putting It Into Practice demonstrates an innovative approach that a student task force took to assist a rural county's sheriff's department deal with domestic violence cases. Anecdotal evidence by social workers in the area reported that the police were not responding to all domestic violence calls, and that those calls that were answered were oftentimes answered at a very slow pace. The task force decided to approach the sheriff to gather more information. What they found were officers who were poorly trained to deal with domestic violence and an overworked staff that saw the same families calling in time and again with no one willing to press charges.

Aside from several other strategies to assist the sheriff's department with training on domestic violence and connecting them with the women's shelter in a neighboring county, students made pocket cards that the police could carry to the residents and quietly slip into the victim's hand if she or he decided (as was often the case) not to press charges or have the

Domestic Violence Pocket Cards—A, Front of Card; B, Back of Card

A

Domestic Violence is a Crime

National Domestic Violence Hotline
1-800-799-SAFE(7233)
1-800-787-3224 (TTD)

B

Safety Plan for Domestic Violence Victims

Safety during an explosive incident

- If an argument seems unavoidable, try to have it in a room or area where you have access to an exit. Try to stay away from the bathroom, kitchen, bedroom or any where else where weapons might be available.
- Practice how to get out of your home safely. Identify which doors, windows, elevator or stairwell would be best.
- Have a packed bag ready and keep it at a relative's or friend's home in order to leave quickly.
- Identify one or more neighbors you can tell about the violence and ask that they call the police if they hear a disturbance coming from your home.
- Device a code word to use with your children, family, friends and neighbors when you need the police.
- Decide and plan for where you will go if you have to leave home (even if you don't think you will need to).
- Use your own instincts and judgement. If the situation is very dangerous, consider giving the abuser what he wants to calm him down.

You have the right to protect yourself until you are out of danger.
- *Always remember-*
YOU DON'T DESERVE TO BE HIT OR BE THREATENED!!!!

Safety When Preparing to Leave

- Open a savings account and/or a credit card in your own name to start to establish or increase your independence. Think of other ways in which you can increase your independence.
- Leave money, an extra set of keys, copies of important documents, extra medicines and clothes with someone you trust so you can leave quickly.
- Determine who would be able to let you stay with them or lend you money.
- Keep the shelter or hotline phone numbers close at hand and keep some change or a calling card on you at all times for emergency phone calls.
- Review your Safety Plan as often as possible in order to plan the safest way to leave your abuser. *REMEMBER -*
- *LEAVING YOUR ABUSER IS THE MOST DANGEROUS TIME!!!!*

What is an Order of Protection?

It is a legal order to protect the victim from further abuse.

How to obtain an order of Protection

- Fill out a petition at the County Court Clerk's office for an order of protection and an ex parte order. They will schedule a court hearing approximately 10 days from petition date. An order is effective for one year.

√ *Be aware that the respondent will be served papers prior to the court date and has the option of participating in the court hearing.*

For More Information ...

24 Hour Emergency Housing & Other Services

Law Enforcement

Emergency	911

City Police (non-emergency)

Greeneville	639-7111
Johnson City	926-5134
Bristol	989-5600
Kingsport	246-9111
Erwin	743-1870
Elizabethton	542-4141

County Sheriff's Department:

Greene	639-3181
Washington	461-1414
Sullivan	323-5121
Carter	543-1850
Unicoi	743-1850

Safe Passage	926-7233
Safe Passage Beeper	461-0268
Abuse Alternatives	652-9093
Safe House	578-3968
CHIPS	742-0022
Contact	926-0144

perpetrator removed. Panels A and B show the small pocket-size card. Panel B show the amount of information that was put on the inside of the card, and that was just the inside cover! They were made by using the columns tab on WordPerfect, making two columns lengthwise and typing the information in the landscape format so the words were sideways on the page. Two cards could be made out of one piece of paper, folded. This gave four small pages that had information front and back. They also had facts about domestic violence, signs of domestic violence, options for victims of domestic violence, an outline of a safety plan, how to obtain an order of protection, and phone numbers for services for victims of domestic violence in nearby areas. All of this on a 2 × 4 inch card that could be slipped into a victim's hand without being seen. The sheriff's department really liked the card, because they felt at a loss to help the women who would call. Because the victims often refused to press charges, and the perpetrator was sometimes present, they did not feel comfortable talking to the officers, and did not know what to say except that they could take them to jail. The pocket cards gave them information they could carry with them in their shirt pocket.

POLICY PRACTICE ONLINE

Before beginning a discussion about using the Internet for policy practice, it is important to think again about the target audience and our strategies in the planning stage. Who are we targeting? How can we best use the Internet to target this agency, representative, or community? If we are going to do a public awareness campaign (see Chapter 7 for more details), for example, is the community connected to the Internet? If we are organizing a grassroots campaign around a policy issue from a low-income area, should we use a strategy that assumes the residents have access to the Internet? These are important questions to ask, because we cannot assume that people have computers, have Internet service, or have access to the Internet.

Having differential access to the Internet and the skills needed to use it refers to an issue known as the *digital divide*. The digital divide is broadly described as the gap between individuals and communities who have access to digital technology and those who do not. Steyaert (2002) outlined how access to technology replicates existing social stratification. If this is still the case, then strategies that attempt to organize poor communities online will not reach their target population. However, the divide in access has been closing as computers and Internet services have become cheaper. Between 2000 and 2005, for example, the Pew Charitable Trust (2006) found that households who use the computer in the United States increased from 62 percent to 70 percent and Internet use climbed from 46 percent to 67 percent during the same period. Rapid Reference 5.1 shows the breakdown by gender, race, and age during these two periods.

It is clear that access to computers and the Internet grew dramatically during the 5-year period between 2000 and 2005. However, it is also clear that there are still up to 42 percent of some populations without access to the Internet, and almost three-fourths of our oldest population lack access to the Internet. In 2006, the Pew survey was replicated, now including income and education in its report. As Rapid Reference 5.2 points out, while the digital divide has clearly become smaller by race and gender, there is a greater divide by age and socioeconomic status. Older Americans are much less likely to use the Internet than younger Americans. Only 53 percent of households with incomes less than $30,000 per year and only 40 percent with less than a high school education use the Internet. Steyaert's (2002) claim of the digital divide following the general stratification of society appears to continue to hold true by economic status. Those with less education are the most likely to make less money, and these two groups used the Internet the least.

There is also growing concern that the digital divide is not just about access. Even though a household may report they use the Internet, the type of use is important. It is not enough to ask whether one has access, but how the Internet is used and what the quality of access is. For example, Riley, Wersma, and Belmarez (2006) report that only 46 percent of students in

≣ *Rapid Reference 5.1*

Computer and Internet Use, 2000–2005 (%)

	2000	2005
Computer Use		
Men	64	71
Women	60	70
Whites	53	71
Blacks	51	66
Hispanics	58	72
18–29	78	84
30–49	74	80
50–64	54	72
65+	20	29
Internet Use		
Men	49	68
Women	44	65
Whites	48	67
Blacks	35	58
Hispanics	40	68
18–29	64	84
30–49	56	76
50–64	36	64
65+	12	27

Adapted from Pew Charitable Trust (2006).

metro Nashville could research term papers or find online information from home during the 2005–2006 school year. In fact, statewide surveys show that in Tennessee, 40 of 140 schools had access levels of less than 50 percent from home.

There should be caution used when deciding when and how to use the

≡ *Rapid Reference 5.2*

Percent Internet Use, by Selected Characteristics, 2006

	Internet Users
Age 18–29	88
Age 65 and older	32
Income less than $30,000 per year	53
Income $75,000 plus	91
Less than high school education	40
College education	91

Adapted from Pew Charitable Trust (2006).

CAUTION

Know your target audience and your stakeholders and discuss the pros and cons of reaching them via the Internet. The digital divide still exists and should be analyzed before attempting to use advanced technology to reach an audience that does not use it.

Internet in policy practice, particularly in terms of lower-income and elderly families. On the other hand, there are new and exciting changes occurring with the Internet that are making policy advocacy strategies more efficient and effective. Keeping in mind the caveats discussed earlier, the creative ways that technology is being used to organize grassroots movements and simplify lobbying and advocacy today are phenomenal.

E-mail Campaigns and Web Sites

E-mail campaigns are probably the most widely used vehicle of Internet policy practice technology today. It is very easy to keep people informed about upcoming events, policy decisions, or to request action via e-mail.

For small nonprofit organizations or for task groups focused on a particular policy issue, e-mail is a cheap and quick way to get information to a large number of people. Many Internet providers offer e-mail accounts and basic web sites free of charge. Because e-mail and the Web are connected, one can attach a web site address that can be directly connected through an e-mail. Web sites can also be registered with various search engines, such as Google, for free. Although free web sites are appealing, your address can get buried under the domain of your service provider. For a small fee (I saw several between $7.00 and $10.00 a month) you can get your own web domain (e.g., www.stopthetoxicwastedump.com).

Web sites can be tools to disseminate information about your cause, your group, or your organization, and also can provide links to other similar organizations. They can be one-way or interactive. Interactive web sites are becoming more popular and advocacy organizations, in particular, increasingly provide direct links to decision makers on their web sites. One interesting example of an interactive web site is www.propeace.net. It provides listservs, blogs, connects to propeace sites in other countries, and has an instant message chat function. These types of web sites are not only good for policy practice activities, but also provide a source of support and communication to people who want to talk about the issues that the web site addresses.

The use of e-mail is becoming a widely used vehicle to communicate with public officials. Since 1998, when I first began to take students to the state capitol to meet with representatives and lobbyists, I have seen the interest in e-mail as an avenue for communication with legislators increase dramatically. In particular, over the last five years, when legislators are asked "what is a good way to communicate with you?" they always list sending an e-mail as one of their primary ways of communicating with their constituents. However, they also say they do not like e-mails that look like a group effort. In fact, I have had several legislators tell me that they treat those e-mails as if they were phoned in calls to support or oppose an issue: they tally them in order of support or opposition, but do not read them. Representatives are interested in constituents who take the time to write individual e-mails, not in forwarded mass form letters. This issue will be taken up in more depth in the next section on listservs.

Listservs and Social Networking

Online social networking involves connecting with other like-minded people around issues that are important to them (Satterfield, 2006). Listservs are a major source of social networking on the Internet. Listservs are e-mail lists that people join because they are interested in an issue. Listservs are among the most useful Internet power tools. Use a listserv in conjunction with your web site to push your message to your target audience and promote traffic to your web site at the same time. Listservs have many different uses and users:

- Associations use listservs to notify their members of meetings and events.
- Special interest groups use listservs to exchange ideas and discuss issues.
- Politicians use listservs to communicate with their constituents.
- Groups with members in diverse locales use listservs to communicate efficiently and economically.

Listservs can be one-way (sends out messages only) or they can be interactive. They can be unmoderated or moderated, meaning that someone looks at the posting before sending it out to ensure that it meets the guidelines of the list. One of the caveats of listservs is that it can fill your e-mail up if you belong to too many lists. Pick the ones that are important to you or your organization and that keep you abreast of your most-needed information. If you find that you are deleting postings without reading them, you should probably unsubscribe from the list.

Some of the listservs and e-groups that I belong to include:

- ETNPRONET, the East Tennessee Progressive Network, which keeps me abreast of local issues affecting my area through an online regional progressive community calendar and online information on organizations working for social justice in my area (www.etnpronet.org/info@etnpronet.org).

- NASW Tennessee legislative alerts, providing alerts for state legislation of interest to social workers, such as what committee a bill is in and who is on the committee to contact (www.naswtn .com/advocacy.htm).
- TrueMajority.org, a grassroots group that monitors upcoming legislation on a federal level (alerts@truemajority.org).
- WorkingFamilies e-activist network, a union-based group that monitors labor and family legislation at the federal level (www .unionvoice.org).
- Working Assets Flash Activist Network, a for-profit long distance phone company that believes in corporate social responsibility and donates 1 percent of long distance calls to progressive nonprofits of your choice (www.workingassets.com).

As you can see, my e-mail gets clogged sometimes. But I have chosen these particular listservs for a reason. I want to keep up with what is going on in my community, so the East Tennessee Progressive Network provides me with the comprehensive tools and web-based resources of its interactive progressive community calendar and organizational directory to keep East Tennessee progressives abreast of local grassroots issues and help build and foster authentic relationships between and among the community. The NASW list provides me with state-level policy tracking, so that I can contact representatives while a bill is still in committee. All NASW members in Tennessee automatically receive legislative updates on national and state-level issues. (Members can indicate they do not wish to receive legislative information and their request is honored.) The web site to sign up as a member is www.socialworkers.org. To view the Tennessee chapter's legislative agenda and key information on specific legislation, go to http://www.naswtn.com/advocacy.htm for information on Tennessee state-level issues, or to http://www.socialworkers.org/advocacy/default

.asp for information on federal issues. Social workers in other states can connect to their local chapter through the national web site listed here.

The last three listservs not only provide updates on legislation that I'm interested in following, but each one uses what Turner (2002) describes as *flash campaigns,* allowing members of the groups to organize quickly around policy issues as they are being debated. Each of these three provides direct links to decision makers on their postings. Because I am a member of each list, they will send me postings that already include my legislator, his or her phone number, and even a form letter that I can simply click "send" and it will be e-mailed for me. However, as I stated earlier, I generally change form letters (along with subject lines) into my own words, so that legislators will actually read it. However, on the federal level, most of the responses from representatives are form letters as well, so my sense is that the local and state representatives are more responsive to personalized e-mails than are federal representatives.

It is also very easy to start a listserv of your own. Yahoo, for example, provides free groups that you can join or start. But Schwartz (2002) warns that although listservs are easy to start, it is much more difficult to get people to join and organize around common goals. He suggests that it is important to moderate the listservs so that people who subscribe have common goals and want to develop strategies around similar issues. He also suggests making the goals clear up front and unsubscribing people who do not share them. Having managed listservs for many years, Schwartz states that people who are interested in working for policy change on a particular issue are not interested in debating it, but to connect with like-minded people to work for change. Unless it is a local issue that is gaining momentum but no one has already organized around it through the Internet, it is likely that an existing list can be used.

CAUTION

Online petitions and form letters are not viewed by public officials nearly as positively as an individualized e-mail. If you choose to use a form letter from a listserv, change the subject line and try to rewrite it in your own words.

It might be more helpful to create a strategy to organize people onto an existing list rather than to start a new one.

Whether you decide to subscribe to an existing list or start your own, the listserv can be used to accomplish a planned change effort, outlined in Chapter 2. It can be used to plan interventions without constantly trying to find times when everyone can meet. It can also include people who are farther away, particularly if you are in a rural area. For example, the East Tennessee Progressive Network utilizes technology to connect people from rural areas, but the issues are still pertaining to the local Appalachian region.

Communication and the Virtual Community

The virtual online community has taken social networking to a new level. Web sites such as Friendster and MySpace are designed to connect people who share common interests. Originally intended as a matchmaking mechanism for youths to find friends, these sites support personal web pages, blogs, and e-messaging all on one person's personal page. The web site itself creates its own directory of people and interests, thereby connecting people with what is known as a *friend of a friend* (FOAF) social network (Satterfield, 2006). When you find someone with similar interests, you can send them a message and ask to be added to their contact list, in turn allowing you to meet other like-minded people on that person's network of friends.

Although these sites were not designed to be political sites in particular, they have, on some level, taken on a life of their own. Nonprofits and others have learned to leverage them to accomplish political goals. MySpace, for example, is an extremely popular site that does not cater to a specific audience. It offers user blogs (an online diary of sorts, where people can post their thoughts on particular topics), message boards, and a free classified ad section. Nonprofits have begun to utilize the site to form groups (listservs), and use the message board to announce upcoming events.

But the most fascinating aspect of MySpace is the friend-of-a-friend format. Because it is one of the most popular sites on the Internet (from 90 million members in July 2006 to 120 million members in October) people can connect in a variety of ways. The most important way is that if you search and find someone who you are connected to or want to be connected to, you can message them and ask them to be your friend. If a person has 25 friends, those 25 friends' web sites are all on the first person's web site.

As I stated earlier, the site was never created for social activism. But it turned out to be an integral part of organizing the national pro-immigration rally that occurred May 1, 2006 (Melber, 2006). Known as a "day without immigrants," hundreds of thousands of Americans rallied on that day to protest congressional debate of a bill designed to crack down on illegal immigrants. *Business Week* magazine reported that the protests were so massive they forced Republican leaders to repudiate a controversial component of a bill that criminalized assistance to illegal immigrants.

How did MySpace have such an impact? The network of young people, in particular, that had been established to discuss social events took a political turn when people started communicating about the upcoming protests and national boycott of businesses. According to an article in *The Nation* by Melber (2006), messages spread among young people who had previously shown little interest in politics. There is really no way to tell how many people joined those marches because of MySpace, but the reporters who have written about it in the *Dallas Morning News* and *The Nation* found thousands of postings in a matter of months. One woman who was trying to get the word out about the issue acquired 400 friends in 2 months. This means that all of her friends had her web site linked to theirs, and all of their friends had friends of their own, so information about an issue spreads exponentially. Furthermore, because MySpace is registered with search engines, such as Google, anyone who searches for the immigration issue will be directed to many of the blogs on MySpace because it is such a popular site. The following Putting It Into Practice further describes this phenomena by describing how one activist, interviewed by *The Nation* in a recent article on the immigration issue (Melber,

Putting It Into Practice

Innovative Uses of Social Networking and Virtual Communities

Carl Webb, a self-proclaimed Internet researcher and political activist, has won the esteemed position of being the first "hit" on Google if you enter his name in the search engine. Why? Because search engines are currently based on popularity, and Carl has had many hits on his MySpace web page, among others. Surprisingly, Carl Webb has 10,000 friends on MySpace. Whenever Carl has something to say, he can go to the MySpace bulletin board and instantly send out postings to all 10,000 friends. I asked Carl how people end up with that many friends. "People want to be your friend because their page comes up whenever anyone looks you up. People can piggy-back off your popularity, taking advantage of a contact." In turn, search engines send out "spiders" or "crawl" through the Internet, picking up tags or keywords to use in searches. Because he has so many contacts, he can post bulletins or write blogs and these come up on the search engine. He decided to join MySpace to use the medium to get his political messages out. He said, "MySpace was originally intended as a matchmaking mechanism for younger people, but people have co-opted the space for other purposes." Has he been successful? In the last few months he has been contacted by the *St. Louis Post-Dispatch* for his antiwar views, *The Nation,* because of his immigration postings, and is currently listed under the Census Bureau's web site search engine. He said that was an unintended contact, because the search engine picked up his name and, because he worked at the Census Bureau, they automatically listed him on the web site. I wouldn't be surprised if he inadvertently helped promote the immigration rally, since he had 7,000 friends on MySpace at the time. *The Nation* article apparently thought so.

2006), has used the virtual community to get out his political messages, receiving quite a bit of publicity in the process.

Posting bulletins on MySpace results in an automatic message sent to all of your friends. In late December 2006 there was a story that was posted about a young woman in Iran who had been sentenced to death for murdering a man who had sexually attacked her. There was a web site with a petition that asked the death sentence be withdrawn and the conviction changed to self defense. My daughter received the bulletin from one of her contacts and reposted it to all of her friends. We watched the number of names on that petition increase to 350,000 in a matter of weeks. In the middle of January 2007 there was a final posting that indicated the petition, which now had more than 500,000 names listed from all around the world, had been given to the United Nations and an appeals court in Iran. The death sentence had been overturned and her conviction was reduced to a lesser conviction related to self defense.

Cell Phones

I would be remiss if I did not include cell phone use in the chapter on technology. The number of cell phone subscribers in the United States reached 159 million in 2003, and climbed to 180 million in 2004 (U.S. Census Bureau, 2004; Baig, 2005). More than 60 percent of Americans have cell phones, and it's not just for talking any more. Cell phones send e-mail, take pictures, connect to the Internet, and have instant messaging. It has become another way to access the Internet without having a computer; the instant messaging capacity was mentioned as part of the organizing effort of the immigration protests described earlier (Melber, 2006).

The importance of cell phones in being digitally connected cannot be underestimated, particularly because of their popularity among young people. It will be interesting to see how the rapid expansion of communication technology affects policy practice efforts in the future. Never before have so many people been connected so rapidly and able to respond to political issues as quickly as they are today.

Policy Practice Resources on the Internet

There are a variety of resources available for policy practice activities on the Internet. Rapid Reference 5.3 divides these into three categories:

≡ *Rapid Reference 5.3*

Suggested Internet Sites for Policy Practice Pursuits

Resources for Policy Practice Activities:

www.grassroots-advocacy.com

www.nfg.org/cotb/39resourcesindex.htm—community organizing toolbox

www.grassrootscampaigns.com/articles

www.candidateshandbook.com—buy or preview books for grassroots campaigns

How to Find Your Legislators, National, State, and Local:

www.vote-smart.org/search/—Project Vote Smart

www.visi.com/juan/congress/—contacting the Congress (also in Spanish)

Policy Analysis and Watchdog Organizations:

www.cbpp.org—Center on Budget and Policy Priorities

www.omb.org—OMB Watch

www.census.gov—Census information

www.truemajority.org—interactive site for policy advocacy on progressive issues

www.urbaninstitute.org—policy analysis of social policies

www.brookings.edu—The Brookings Institute, policy analysis of social policies

learning tools, access to policymakers, and information. These are a small sample of the types of policy practice resources now available. Learning tools provide skills and methods for various planned change activities, including how to advocate on a grassroots level, how to run a political campaign, and how to organize communities.

Finding out who your legislators are has become much easier with the Internet. The two web sites offered in Rapid Reference 5.3 provide two advantages. Contact Congress provides a letter format so that after you search for your legislator by zip code, you can also contact them. Vote Smart allows one to search for his or her local representatives as well as state and federal legislators.

Accessing information on the Internet has provided opportunities that were virtually impossible just 20 years ago. Government statistics are readily available on any number of populations and social problems. Think tanks and watchdog organizations supply a plethora of different reports on policies of interest. Rapid Reference 5.3 provides a small sampling of what can now be accessed through the Internet in a few hours, in what would have taken weeks or months prior to the World Wide Web.

The Future of Free Speech on the Internet

No matter which side of an issue you are on, the Internet provides a truly democratic outlet for views of all kinds. The Internet presently has little control over what is published. With the inception of blogs, virtual communities, web sites, listservs, and e-mail, the Internet has become a vehicle for free speech. Currently there have been attempts to control the information on the Internet by broadband providers, such as AT&T, Comcast, and Verizon. Congress is currently considering a major overhaul of the Telecommunications Act. The Senate bill (S. 2686), like the House version that has already passed, would allow broadband providers to prioritize traffic on their networks. This can be done in two ways, through the speed at which broadband providers allow web sites to be accessed and through prioritizing access to their search engines. The bill does not bar broadband providers from favoring their own online traffic or making deals with Internet companies to provide faster service to their customers (Tessler, 2006). But Internet companies, including Microsoft, Google, and Yahoo! argue that providers could either favor or discriminate against Internet traffic without some form of protection of net neutrality.

The term *net neutrality* means that all users can access the content on the Internet without control or ownership of content. Search engines, for example, order their hits by the popularity of the web site, not by who spends more money. Although amendments were offered that provided clear guidelines for net neutrality, they have not made it past committee. Net neutrality language is intended to ensure that phone and cable companies cannot use their control over the broadband market to discriminate against online competitors or to demand a premium for fast, reliable access to consumers. Republican Senator Olympia Snow warned that the bill in its current form could turn phone and cable companies into the gatekeepers of the Internet, creating a class system of sorts between small, poor organizations and large, rich corporations and their access to speed and availability of content.

At this writing, it does not appear that this bill has the votes to pass in 2006. However, it is interesting that while researching this chapter, a new policy advocacy group, called "Save the Internet Coalition" emerged on the Web and gathered more than one million signatures on e-mail petitions, which they delivered to Congress to try to kill the bill or have it amended. Their coalition tagged onto the TrueMajority listserv to gather support. After the vote was tied in committee, the coalition sent an e-mail that said, "Although it doesn't look like they have the support, here is the position of your senators on this issue." They provided my senators' names, their position, and their phone numbers. One of the realities of legislative policy practice, which we will go over in more detail in Chapter 8, is that there needs to be support for an issue both at the grassroots level and at the lobbying level in Congress. Representatives need to see that their constituents are paying attention to how they vote. Even though big companies, such as Yahoo! and Microsoft, are working at the federal level, it is important for representatives to hear from their constituents, since we ultimately vote for them. This was a good example of using technology to get grassroots support for an issue.

SUMMARY

The technology revolution is evolving so fast that there may be a new, favorite social network by the time this goes to press. The ease with which computers can connect people from across the globe is unprecedented and makes practicing online policy practice an exciting prospect. However, the digital divide continues to widen—for poor and aged communities, in particular—and that is only in the United States. Thus, as with any planned change effort, using the Internet or computer in general for policy practice must be looked at in the broader scope of the systems we wish to target and the grassroots populations we wish to include in our effort. These systems will be discussed in much greater detail in Chapters 7 through 10. For now, it is important to see the computer and the Internet as strategies that can be used across target systems for a variety of strategic interventions.

TEST YOURSELF

1. Go to www.yahoo.com. If you do not already have an e-mail account, create one for yourself.

2. Go through the web site at Yahoo! and look through the groups to see what kind of groups are already on the web site.

3. Go to the personal web site portal, Geocities.com, and create a free personal web page for yourself. Put in your favorite url web addresses when they prompt you.

4. Alternatively, go to www.MySpace.com. Sign up. Fill in the personal information. It will give you a web page. Fill it in as you like.

5. Click on the "my blog" and write your thoughts.

6. Pick a resource from Rapid Reference 5.3 and go to that web site to see what kinds of information they provide.

7. Go to either Vote Smart or Contacting Congress (Rapid Reference 5.3) and find out who your legislators are.

8. Using a word processing application, utilize the directions in this chapter to create a brochure or newsletter.

9. What are three potential consequences of the digital divide?

10. Describe what net neutrality means and give one example of what might happen if the Internet is not neutral?

Six

ESSENTIALS OF INTEREST GROUP POLITICS: COALITION BUILDING AND TASK FORCE DEVELOPMENT

Three fundamental items are needed by citizens in order to develop enough political power to influence change in any system: information, people, and coordinated activity. People need information in order to understand the nature of the problem, to decide how to propose a change, to understand both sides of an issue, and to contemplate intended and unintended consequences of the actions they choose to implement. We also need to be part of a larger group. Sometimes change can only occur with a significant amount of power, which more than one individual or organization can bring to the table. That is why organized groups are so important. They bring together numbers of people interested in the same issue and provide resources to accumulate information and create widespread action around an issue.

This widespread coordination of people around a political issue has been called *interest group politics*. Often, when we think of interest group politics, we think of large corporate lobbying groups that may not have citizens' best interests in mind. But there are many interest groups that work for the betterment of society as a whole. Hoefer (2001) calls these "human services interest groups," which work together to expand social programs and to ensure social and economic justice. They are also known as citizen groups and public interest groups.

The influence of citizen/public interest groups has been severely underestimated. First, there has been an increase in citizen groups over time, and this rise has had an impact on the way policy is formulated, making the entire policymaking process more participatory. They have played a critical role in legislative decision making, the implementation of laws, and opening up the court system. In the human services, these may include nonprofit organizations, professional associations, coalitions, and citizen task forces. Interest groups have largely been analyzed for their effectiveness on the national level, but there is new and compelling evidence that interest groups are important and effective at local and state levels as well (Hoefer, 2005; Tichenor & Harris, 2002/2003).

Professional associations, such as the National Association of Social Workers (NASW), are organized at local, state, and national levels. They are politically active in a number of ways. They have political action committees (PACs) that endorse candidates for elections, and legislative committees that track legislation, find sponsors for legislation, lobby, and support or oppose existing legislation. Because professional associations are most often interested in lobbying in the state and federal arena, and because they are, by and large, already organized by virtue of their membership, I will reserve the bulk of the discussion on change strategies of professional associations at the legislative level to Chapter 8. However, much of the discussion in this chapter on effective decision making, collaboration, and consensus building is pertinent to all groups working in policy practice.

Nonprofit organizations have grown in their influence over the last 20 years, largely through collective efforts with other organizations and with coalitions they may belong to, and in combining their efforts in more short term, ad hoc collaborative efforts on specific issues (Gray & Lowery, 2001). Coalitions of nonprofits and citizens are more effective than single organizations. They work on issues at many systems levels, from addressing local community problems to state and national legislation.

Unlike professional associations, coalitions and citizen task groups are not already organized through a member association. They form around specific issues or populations. While they can be very effective change agents, they also face many challenges in organizing and maintaining their membership and focus. This chapter will focus on the skills needed to develop and maintain effective coalitions and citizen task forces that can be used across a spectrum of potential policy targets, from communities and local organizations to state and national government.

In his research on highly effective groups, Hoefer (2001) found six tactics that differentiated highly effective from less effective interest groups. He found that highly effective groups work with legislators on policy formulation, aid in the election of candidates, work with government agencies on policy implementation, and pursue issues in court. These four tactics will be discussed in depth in Chapters 8, 9, and 10. Fifth, he found that highly effective groups use the media to influence public opinion, which we discussed in Chapter 4. Finally, he found that highly effective groups developed consensus among different interest groups around issues. This is important, because policymakers at all levels of government prefer that differences between stakeholders be worked out prior to a vote on the issue. When organizations and coalitions can build consensus around issues, they are more likely to win that issue. If different groups cannot completely agree, then it is better for the groups to come together to find some middle ground that they can agree on, rather than force a vote without agreement. Policymakers prefer "near-unanimity among policy combatants before voting" (p. 8). Therefore, interest groups, whether they are task groups, organizations, or coalitions, must be proactive, know the different sides of issues, know who is on what side of the issue, and open the lines of communications with varying stakeholders in order to be successful in getting policy changed.

Berry (1999) finds that the increase in citizen groups has prompted policymaking to move away from a small, closed group of key government officials and favored lobbyists to a much broader policymaking community. The importance of coalitions and consensus building among coalitions cannot be underestimated. Even organizations that do not normally work on political issues, or are not involved with a particular network of coalitions, can easily combine forces temporarily to work on a single issue that will benefit both groups. The following Putting It Into Practice explores this phenomenon with my own experience with a pharmaceutical

Putting It Into Practice

Strange Bedfellows in the Policy Process

I had been doing research on Tennessee's Medicaid Managed Care program, called TennCare, since its inception in 1994. When Tennessee began to cut back their TennCare services in 1996, there was much media speculation as to the impact that would have on various populations desperately needing care. I decided to do follow-up research on people who were beginning to have difficulties with TennCare to assess, in more depth, where the breakdown in the system was occurring. I approached a grassroots organization that I had worked with on a previous health care study in 1995 and asked them if they could help me locate neighbors in their area who were having difficulty with TennCare. We teamed up together; they needed good research to support their political agenda to assist residents with health care needs and gain credibility through an academic study; I needed access to people who were difficult to locate. Through a participatory-style research project, we worked together to locate 40 TennCare recipients who were experiencing difficulties with various aspects of the TennCare system. After I finished my analysis, I released a report to the organization of my findings. They immediately called a press conference to relay the new research on the difficulties the new cutbacks were creating for recipients.

One of my findings (there were several) was that changing the drug formulary resulted in people being switched from their current prescriptions to cheaper medicine to try to control the rising costs of the program. This, in and of itself, was not a problem. The problem lay in the fact that many of these people had already tried the medicine that the new formulary suggested they switch to. There was a process for people to appeal, but the process took time, and in the meantime, put people at risk for a number of adverse physical and mental problems.

Interestingly, at the same time that my report was being publicized, there was a pharmaceutical interest group that was heavily lobbying the state to have their drugs reinstated on the formulary. Out of the blue, I received a call from their lobbyist, asking if I could testify before the TennCare Oversight Committee on such and such a day. He would be testifying the same day right after I was finished. More than a little surprised, I asked how I could contact the chair to see if I could be invited—"no problem," he said, he had already taken care of it. Now more than a little suspicious,

I asked him if he could fax me his testimony. He did, and I understood. He had taken my report and his testimony was full of references to my academic study, which supported his organization's desire to increase the list of pharmaceuticals on the formulary. My study had not only given the grassroots advocacy group the legitimacy they needed to get their message out to the public, but it had also given the pharmaceutical company additional leverage to add their medications back onto the formulary. What is the lesson from this? As I have heard in the political arena many times, there are no permanent allies and no permanent enemies. I would have never thought I would team up with both a grassroots organization and a large pharmaceutical lobby on the same issue, but that is what it took to get back needed services to people who were desperate for their medication. Without either group, the effort might have failed.

interest group, a local grassroots advocacy group for Medicaid Managed Care access, and my own academic research.

DEFINING TASK FORCES AND COALITIONS

While task forces are groups of people who come together with a specific issue in mind, coalitions are strategic groups designed to enhance the leverage of various organizations with regard to some problem or set of issues. Both coalitions and task forces can (a) advocate for changes in existing policy, (b) advocate for passage of new legislation, (c) track the implementation of new policies into programs, and (d) communicate with large numbers of people in order to mobilize them into action.

Task forces are generally small groups of people who form to address a specific problem or issue. I have very often seen groups as small as four or six people make the difference in a policy passing or failing. Particularly at the local and state level, where a majority of decisions are made that affect our daily lives, task forces can have great influence. I have worked for over 10 years with small student task forces on issues in the community, from changing local handicapped accessibility of businesses to adding amendments to state laws, and have seen major successes come from small groups. As Margaret Mead so succinctly said, "Never doubt that a small group of committed citizens can change the world." In a time when citizen apathy is at one of the highest points in recent history, it is important to know that we really can make a difference, particularly around issues that affect us on a daily basis.

In fact, I want to make the point that even one or two people can make a difference. I think this is something that most people really do not believe. For example, in a discussion with Senator Tim Burchett (R-TN) about lobbying and how he makes decisions about the thousands of bills that cross his desk every legislative session, he said that for most issues he gets his information from varying interest group lobbyists, because they are always there providing statistics and other pertinent information on legislation. But what gets his attention the most is when he hears from constituents back home. He said, "If I get three phone calls [from home] that's a groundswell, and I pay attention."

Another example that shows the importance of each person's influence to make changes is when an ordinance was being considered to create a curfew in the county where I live. The county commission was considering an ordinance that would have instituted what I considered an overly restrictive curfew for teenagers. I called my two county commissioners about the issue. Even though it had been in the paper and on the news, both of my commissioners told me I was the first parent who had called. I talked with them about kids who work late, or teens who wanted to hit the late show, which would put them out past curfew on their way home. I just basically talked about my own experiences as a parent. Neither commissioner had teenagers. After our discussion they thanked me sincerely for the input. That ordinance did not pass, and when I looked at the vote, I felt that I had made a difference. One person.

While task forces are generally groups of individuals that form around a specific problem, coalitions are larger groups that can have both organizations and individuals as members, can be permanent or temporary, and can focus on specific issues, populations, or pieces of legislation. The exact nature of the coalition and what the goals are should be considered when deciding what type of coalition will be most effective for the problem at hand. For example, ad hoc coalitions form around a specific issue or piece of legislation and tend to be relatively short term, while formal coalitions are highly structured, may be more effective, but are also more costly. They have formal structures, bylaws, need financial contributions, and have elected leaders.

According to Mizrahi and Rosenthal (2001), coalitions that focus on social change commit to an agreed-upon purpose and shared decision making to influence an external institution or target. Member organizations maintain their own autonomy as organizations, but come together around policy issues in an attempt to influence public opinion, create new policies, or oppose proposed policies. First, let's look at how to successfully build and maintain coalitions. Then we will look at how to manage potential conflict in groups.

Building Coalitions

Building coalitions requires a group of people who share the same concern for a problem or an issue. Usually these people or organizations are being personally or professionally affected by a problem. This core group of people will do the initial work to strategize how to organize the coalition, how to get others interested, and to decide which other organizations and key stakeholders should be approached to become involved. The strategy should include evidence that the issue is best solved through a coalition rather than through an existing organization. A thorough assessment of what resources will be needed for the coalition to reach its goals must be determined, and a decision made as to the type of coalition that will best serve to alleviate the problem or change the policy. After the initial decisions about the type of coalition that is needed and who would be important organizations and stakeholders to be members of it, the core group begins to make contacts with potential members, ask for their input, and attempt to get them involved and invested in the coalition.

It is natural to want to increase the size of the coalition as much as possible. We know that there is power in numbers. But it is not a good idea to broaden the goals of the coalition simply to include more people. This will weaken your position, and personal agendas may begin to compete with the larger purpose of the coalition. Some of the problems with coalition building are that organizations fear a lack of autonomy and are hesitant to commit resources during a time of increased uneasiness about funding. Cutbacks and unpredictable distribution of resources at the local level undermine the cooperative relationship that exists among many human service organizations.

Even after a coalition has formed, there are challenges in reaching its goals. Some external challenges are largely beyond the control of the coalition, such as timing, the political climate, and the target system that the coalition is dealing with. If the coalition is an ad hoc effort forming around a legislative issue, for example, there needs to be enough time for the coalition to agree on what actions to take before decisions have to be made. Time for groups to process is very important, and the shorter the time period between the emergence of an issue and when the final action is necessary, the greater the likelihood that conflict will begin to develop within the coalition.

On the flip side, coalitions may come together with the expectation that change can occur relatively rapidly. But patience is a virtue in the policy process, no matter if it is a local government, an organization, or a legislative body. There are windows of opportunity for change and the coalition may need to wait for one of these windows to open. The coalition must be ready to move into action when the political climate begins to show signs that it is ready for change.

Internal Factors for Successful Coalitions

Some of the challenges of creating and maintaining coalitions have been outlined earlier. Many of these are external, such as timing and political climate, but there are important internal factors that influence whether a coalition will be successful in achieving its goals. Mizrahi and Rosenthal

(2001) found that the coalitions' ability to sustain participation and maintain their efforts, particularly with a challenging external environment, can be difficult.

While it is understood that not all members will work as much as others, and that each organization has only a certain amount of resources to give to the effort, the real challenge is to learn how to minimize the inherent tension and conflict when people come together with different personalities, needs, and experiences, even if they believe in the same goal. Much of this work must be done by the leaders of the coalition, who are the few who will do most of the work and take much of the responsibility. Some important internal elements of successful leadership are outlined in Rapid Reference 6.1.

Rapid Reference 6.1

Elements of Successful Coalition Leadership

- Commitment
- Competent leadership
- Coalition unity
- Equitable decision-making structure/process
- Mutual trust and respect
- Shared responsibility and ownership

BUILDING GROUP CONSENSUS IN THE POLICY PRACTICE PROCESS

Even though a group comes together around an issue, that does not mean there will not be differences of opinion on what policy change is necessary and how to effect that change. Having the skills to enhance collaboration and consensus building in task forces and coalitions and learning to respect the process of group decision making is part of the participatory process. Much like the skills in community building, small-group techniques for trust, collaboration, and consensus building are important. Even if a group has come together and agreed upon the problem to be addressed and the goals of the effort, multiple personalities and different ideas about how to accomplish the task are bound to create conflict. The following sections will provide some specific skills to assist in building consensus and decreasing conflict in small groups.

Enhancing Collaboration and Consensus Building

Not all issues are appropriate for a consensus-based approach to decision making. Indeed, groups working on policy change could just as easily vote on how they want to proceed, what interventions they want to undertake, and so on. But the most effective groups are the ones where all members support the decisions that have been made. If a vote is needed, then not all members support the decision and likely will not be as invested in the process to work for that particular change. Consensus is achieved through discussion, so as to combine the best ideas of all members. Thus the final outcome incorporates some pieces of everyone's point of view. All members agree with the group's position or are close enough that they can support it. For policy practice groups, people have joined because they have a common interest around an issue that is important to them. Thus, the consensus model is appropriate for groups focusing on policy change. Because it is participatory, the likelihood that members will do agreed-upon tasks is also greater, because each person can see part of his or her view in the final decision.

For consensus to work, the group needs to agree on the definition of the problem, have a sense of ownership of the process, and have a sense of trust in the process and in their group members. Carpenter (1999) delineates six steps in approaching consensus building.

1. Agree on the definition of the problem.
2. Agree on ground rules.
3. Share information on each person's experiences and how he or she views the context of the problem.
4. Develop options (in each step of the process).
5. Evaluate options, using agreed-upon criteria.
6. Seek agreement on the entire change package that all parties can support.

Whereas the planning process in Chapter 2 provides the steps in the change effort, including looking at different options for interventions to fulfill the objectives of the policy change, the consensus model requires that every step of the process, from goal setting to taking action, must be agreed upon through sharing information, developing and evaluating options, and seeking agreement that everyone supports.

Ground rules can cover behavioral expectations, substantive issues, and procedural issues. Behavioral expectations can include such things as respecting others' opinions, trying not to dominate discussions, promoting an open and supportive climate, and making sure that all people have the opportunity to participate. Substantive issues include agreeing on which issues will be addressed. This may seem obvious, but often groups may try to take on too broad a range of issues. Narrowing the issues will focus the group and decrease the likelihood of conflict later on. Finally, procedural issues focus on how decisions will be made and how information will be shared. Setting ground rules is important because it guides the process and structures the group.

Consensus is best reached when everyone has the same understanding of a problem. Therefore the context of a problem, how people see it from their own perspective, is essential in building consensus and trust in a group. Taking the time up front to share personal experiences, as well as information related to the problem, allows people to understand each other's perspectives, build trust, and create greater participation among group members.

The better the relationships and the greater the trust of the group up front, the more participants can focus on the substantive policy issue at hand. If the relationships within the group are strained for some reason, then relationship building must be integrated into the consensus-building process. This is when ground rules include such things as behavioral expectations to encourage positive interactions, sharing stories and personal histories, and allowing time for informal conversation and relationship building.

Making Decisions in Small Groups: Small-Group Techniques

There are several ways to enhance decision making in focus groups and coalitions. First there must be a safe environment for the generation of ideas and the stimulation of creative thinking. It is important that all members have an equal chance to participate and that verbal monopolizing be controlled. Here are two techniques that increase participation and generation of ideas.

Brainstorming: Encourages *all* ideas! Nothing is too simple, too difficult, or crazy. Brainstorming encourages group members to build on the ideas of others or to combine them in creative ways. The main principle of brainstorming is that there is no evaluation of the ideas brought out during the brainstorming process. There should be no criticism of ideas, no laughing, and no positive or negative reactions are permitted. Members are asked to think outside the box, even if it seems too wild to work. The facilitator or recorder uses charts or butcher paper to write down the ideas and posts the paper on the wall. Evaluation takes place after the group has listed as many ideas as possible. It is a good idea to take a break between brainstorming and evaluation. In evaluating each idea have some criteria set up, and think critically in terms of the pros and cons of adopting each idea. Rapid Reference 6.2 lists the principles of brainstorming.

If the group has several people who are more outspoken, it may present obstacles to brainstorming. In this case, variations can be used. Galanes, Adams, and Brilhart (2004) suggest that in-

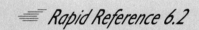

Rapid Reference 6.2

The Principles of Brainstorming

- Problem to solve
- Members of group encouraged to generate as many solutions as possible
- No evaluation permitted
- Quantity sought, innovation encouraged, and may build on others' ideas
- All ideas charted so others can see them
- All ideas evaluated at a different time

dividuals write down their ideas and then transfer them to wall charts. If people feel inhibited for any reason, ideas can be presented on paper anonymously before being transferred to the larger list of ideas. The facilitator is critical in

CAUTION

The facilitator is important in the brainstorming process and allows no judgments of the ideas during the idea-creation phase.

the brainstorming process, to make sure that ground rules are followed, that everyone has a chance to participate, and that no value comments are made.

The assumption behind brainstorming is that group members have knowledge of the issue. The size of the group should be between 5 and 15 people and the time allotted for brainstorming, depending on the size of the group, is generally 15 to 30 minutes. The role of the group leader is to define the problem, stimulate ideas, prevent group members from making evaluative comments during the brainstorming session, keep the group on track, and end the discussion. A recorder should be chosen who places all of the ideas on a chart or butcher paper.

Nominal Group Technique: In this group decision-making technique, there is minimal interaction among group members. Nominal Group Technique (NGT) merges individual ideas into *quality group decisions.* Nominal Group Technique is useful when the group wants to identify a list of problems or generate many solutions, establish priorities of either problems or solutions, and ensure that all members have opportunities to share their ideas. Nominal Group Technique gained popularity because of the uneven participation patterns that may occur in roundtable discussions and brainstorming sessions (Cragan, Wright, & Kasch, 2004).

In NGT, members write their ideas down without interacting with others, and then their ideas are recorded round-robin style on charts. After all ideas are listed, ideas can be clarified, but not verbally evaluated. Each member rank orders the ideas by his or her top choices. This can be put on cards or members can be given stickers which they stick next to their favorite choices.

The assumption of NGT is that ideas that emerge in a group are superior to the ideas of one person. The size of the group should be between 6 and 10 members and the meeting takes between 30 and 45 minutes. The role of the group leader is similar to brainstorming. When a group is attempting to break out into task groups, or is trying to determine potential objectives to meet the goals of a policy intervention, NGT is appropriate to pare down ideas and see how similar members' interests are (see Rapid Reference 6.3).

I use NGT in the classroom when students must decide which policy issues they want to work on in groups. The class uses a recorder to generate all ideas on a chalkboard. Class members can put as many ideas down as they want. After all the potential ideas are on the board, I will usually go around the room and ask each person to now give his or her top three policy problems of interest, and the recorder puts a mark by the top choices for each person. Potential projects that no one has rated are erased. This pares down the ideas significantly. Now that there is a more manageable list, an evaluative discussion can ensue to specify the ideas more explicitly, looking at goals and potential target systems. After that discussion, all

≡ Rapid Reference 6.3

Nominal Group Technique

- Each member writes all ideas down.
- Go around the table and record each idea onto a chart.
- Each item is clarified but not evaluated.
- Each member rank orders her or his favorite ideas (up to three).
- Items not chosen are removed.
- Evaluate and discuss remaining items.
- Members vote a second time for their top choice from the remaining items.

previous marks are erased and the class is again asked to give their choice, only this time it is their number one choice out of the policy projects left. Oftentimes, students have analyzed these enough that natural groups emerge from the remaining topics. It is helpful to begin with their top three choices, because as they see groups forming on the last round, one of the remaining groups is generally in their top three interests. Although this group project may not have been their first choice, it is in their interest area and thus they are generally satisfied with the outcome.

Avoiding and Resolving Conflict in Groups

There are several barriers to building consensus in groups, including lack of trust, inflexible positions, unwillingness to communicate, lack of clear communication, and trying to resolve too many issues, leading to frustration and disengagement. Many of these barriers can be prevented or resolved through good leadership skills by the facilitator of the meetings. Facilitation is the impartial management of meetings, designed to enable participants to focus on the substantive issues and goals (Elliott, 1999). A good facilitator works to incorporate all points of view, coordinate and integrate the ideas of the group, and work toward agreements that all can support.

The importance of learning how to facilitate group meetings cannot be overstated. We have all been to poorly run meetings where we have left feeling frustrated and thinking we just wasted our time. In poorly run meetings, the purpose and agenda are not clearly defined, a few outspoken people are allowed to dominate the discussion; members may become angry or insult others who disagree with their views. Discussions can run on aimlessly. All of these issues can be addressed by the facilitator of the meeting. It is important to provide room for process and participation, and to have a structure for decision making. Even the spatial setup of the room can be important in ensuring that people feel free to speak.

Strauss (1999) outlines the building blocks for successful meetings. Effective meetings follow these guidelines:

- They are conducted through collaboration.
- They offer carefully managed opportunities for discussion, participation, and decision making.
- They include clear roles and responsibilities for group members.
- The facilitators are prepared.
- Agendas are planned ahead of the meeting.
- Facilitators model appropriate behaviors and problem-solving skills.

The facilitator's role is very important because she or he guides the process, makes sure all people have a chance to be heard, and offers suggestions on when to move on. The facilitator is also responsible for planning the meeting, setting up the room, and arranging the physical space. Physical space is important, as it leads to more or less participation. The room should be set up in a semicircle, with plenty of wall space for the collection of ideas. Effective facilitators remember that the job of reaching consensus belongs to the group. Facilitators only manage the process. It is the group's responsibility to reach consensus.

When groups experience conflict it is likely that they lack trust. Trust is essential for groups to work cohesively together: Galanes, Adams, and Brilhart (2004) suggest there are three important principles that build trust in groups:

1. Working together to understand each other. This includes making sure that each person understands another's position before disagreeing and allowing others to disagree with you without making them feel inadequate.
2. Communication. Includes not only communicating in a way that enhances others' self-concept, but also encouraging people to explain themselves and actively listen to others' opinions.
3. Being a responsible group member. Treat others with the same respect that you desire and follow the ground rules set up by the group.

When facilitating a group, it is important to confront members who treat others with disrespect or otherwise break the group's trust. They ensure that all members have the ability to participate without fear or verbal intimidation. Remember, we are all on the same team and are working for the same goal. While we respect the contribution of each group member, if disrespectful behavior is allowed to continue, it could break the task group's ability to work effectively toward their goal.

People who see conflict as inherently bad will try to avoid it. Avoiding conflict, however, may lead to even greater dysfunction than embracing it, because there is a greater likelihood of nonparticipation and passive-aggressive behavior. This occurs when conflict goes unresolved. Good conflict is constructive.

1. Acknowledge that conflict exists.
2. Search for common ground relating to goals.
3. Seek to understand the different perspectives of the disagreement.
4. Attack the issue, not each other.
5. Develop a plan—what each person may do to help solve the problem.

Cultural Aspects of Conflict

Beliefs about the nature of conflict and how to handle it may be influenced by diverse cultures. In the United States, this diversity may include class, race, religion, gender, and sexual orientation, among others. As the world becomes more integrated and global policies become more pertinent at home, we will increasingly work in policy development with cultures outside of our own country as well. Individual versus collectivist cultural differences see conflict very differently, for instance (Cragan, Wright, & Kasch, 2004). Collectivist cultures encourage more collaborative strategies to resolve group conflict, while more individualistic cultures are inclined to use more direct confrontation to address conflict.

Culturally diverse groups can benefit from the differing perspectives group members bring, or they can allow their differences to fuel conflict and prevent group cohesion. While there are more challenges working in diverse groups, cohesive groups that are diverse are more likely to come up with more creative solutions than homogenous groups. Therefore, it is important to initially take a collectivist approach, getting to know one another, sharing perspectives, and spending time building understanding and trust before getting down to the task at hand.

The Importance of Constructive Conflict

It is obvious from the preceding discussion that some conflict is inevitable and may, in fact, be constructive. Indeed, Cragan, Wright, and Kasch (2004) suggest that conflict is important to avoid group-think—"the greater the threats to the self esteem of members [to disagree], the greater will be their inclination to resort to agreement at the expense of critical thinking" (p. 274). Therefore, it is important to keep critical comments, intimidation, and other unproductive behaviors out of the group dynamic. Just as with seeking collaboration, the use of ground rules is important for avoiding unproductive conflict. Suffice it to say, conflict is disagreement, and disagreement is not necessarily bad—it is the way in which people voice that disagreement that is important.

Ting-Toomey and Oetzel (2001) detail useful constructive conflict skills:

- Mindful observation—observe verbal and nonverbal signals exchanged in conflict. Engage in dialogue, respecting differences, suspending evaluation.
- Mindful listening—often we don't hear others when we engage in conflict. Verbal summarizing of other's thoughts can assist in making sure members are listening.
- Mindful reframing—how one frames the conflict may change how he or she responds to it.
- Collaborative dialogue—discovers common ground, shared power. Discuss, don't dominate.
- Focus on the process for now, not the outcome.

If conflict becomes too entrenched in your group and facilitation, beyond what we have discussed here, is needed, the *Conflict Resolution Toolbox* by Gary Furlong (2005) provides several conflict intervention models, two of which are particularly salient for task forces or coalitions working on policy issues. The Dynamics of Trust model uses attribution theory to look at how people have attributed the conflicts to others: either situational, beyond that person's control; intrinsic, part of his or her nature; or intentional, meaning the other person is attributed to being hostile on purpose. The more that a person attributes the conflict from situational to intentional, the less trust there is, and thus, the more conflict. The facilitator goes through a series of steps to see how each party attributes the conflict, and then begins to gently challenge the assumptions of each person's perceptions and shares perceptions and information with each party about the other. The assumption behind this model is that it takes two (or more) people to create a conflict, and generally misperceptions, miscommunication, and thoughtless behavior lead to unproductive conflict. As people begin to understand each other then they can work toward building productive discourse and eventually trust.

A second model in the *Toolbox* that extends the trust model is the Dimensions model. This one extends the idea of simply changing our cognitive perceptions of the conflict to dealing with behaviors and emotions as well. The Dimensions model works under the assumption that even though conflict may be resolved cognitively, there may be underlying emotions that are unresolved and can easily trigger past, negative behaviors. My suggestion is that if your group becomes so entrenched in conflict, it is worth hiring a facilitator who specializes in group conflict intervention. If you are working with a small task force and do not have the resources for an outside person, I suggest finding a person who is viewed as neutral within the group to serve as facilitator and use the interventions outlined in the *Toolbox* to work on the issues within the group. The leadership skills discussed earlier must be within the repertoire of skills that the person who will facilitate has, however. It is not enough to be seen as neutral; good leadership qualities are essential. She or he must be able to create appropriate ground rules, encourage participation, and provide a safe environment to address concerns.

SUMMARY

This chapter outlined the importance of interest groups in policy practice. Greater numbers equate to greater power. But task forces and coalitions are only as effective as the consensus they share about the issue. Although it does not take a large number of people to make a difference in the political arena, it does require a group of people who share the goals and objectives of the policy practice project. Conflict can arise when people see the process to achieve those goals differently, but there are ways to manage conflict. It takes time, but it is worth the effort to have a functional group. It takes much more time to constantly try to contain infighting of group members, and the outcomes will not be as successful.

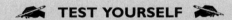

TEST YOURSELF

You want to organize a coalition to support stronger domestic violence legislation that has been proposed for the next legislative session. You currently work at a domestic violence shelter, so you already have various contacts in the community.

1. What stakeholders might be interested in this issue in your community?

2. What type of coalition should you try to create?

3. What issues should you consider when creating the coalition?

4. What characteristics should you look for to form a core group of people to help build the coalition?

5. What are one internal and one external challenge that your coalition may face?

You have a committed task force working on a project to redevelop a blighted area in your city. Each member comes with important expertise that is essential for the effective planning of your project. But some members of the group seem to take over the conversation, and others rarely say a word.

1. What can you do to ensure that all group members have the opportunity to participate equally?
2. Why is good leadership important in increasing participation?
3. How is consensus different from majority rule?
4. What are the principles of brainstorming?
5. How is brainstorming different from nominal group technique?

Seven

ESSENTIALS OF COMMUNITY-BASED POLICY PRACTICE

Practicing policy from a community-based perspective can involve a diverse range of target systems and intervention strategies, some of which we have covered in previous chapters. This chapter will identify several target populations for community-based policy practice and discuss appropriate strategies to increase public awareness about problems, advocate for changes in existing policy, or develop new policies at the local or regional level. This chapter also provides information on working on grassroots campaigns for local elections.

It is the intention of this chapter to address two issues: one, how much of our lives is influenced by local policy, and two, what a difference we can make in a broad range of policies right in our own community. While it often seems like many policy decisions are out of our reach, there is actually a great deal that we can influence locally, some in our neighborhoods and communities and some at the state and national level. As previous chapters have discussed, devolution has taken much of the policymaking decisions down to state and local levels. While it has its drawbacks, one thing is certain: We are closer to policy making than ever before.

Community-based policy practice projects require grassroots participation. Thus, activities are undertaken by the community, as opposed to a lobbyist, for example. Grassroots or community-based policy practice includes many different activities, from organizing groups of citizens to act on local issues or problems to communicating ideas and opinions to government officials. In this book, community-based policy practice is defined as "involving people at the local level in supporting or recommending a cause or policy." Therefore, although the target system can be anything from the local community to a national legislator, the action is taken by people at the local level, rather than lobbyists, political action committees, or membership organizations. This chapter will focus on techniques that individuals and small groups can use to inform the local community of issues confronting them and to influence policy at multiple systems levels.

COMMUNITY AWARENESS CAMPAIGNS

When a problem is first identified or is not receiving much public attention, it may be more strategic to undertake an awareness campaign rather than try to get a policy changed without public knowledge. Community (or public) awareness campaigns are especially valuable when there is a high likelihood that the public will support your issue. This may sound obvious, but with any change strategy, it is important to explore the pros and cons of using a community awareness campaign. Interventions for public awareness are best used when there is a new problem in the community, or a policy is being proposed or implemented, of which the general public is unaware. Community awareness campaigns can also be targeted to a certain population. This is appropriate if the target system is a small subset of the general population, or if support for the topic is divided enough that reaching the entire population might create opposition to your goal. Examples of potentially divisive issues that have recently cropped up on political agendas where targeted awareness campaigns may be most appropriate include issues such as gay and lesbian adoption, emergency contraceptives, and parental permission to use birth control. Both general community awareness campaigns and targeted campaigns will be discussed in this section.

There is little information in the literature on how to create effective community awareness programs. A 2002 report by the General Accounting Office (GAO) found that using previous research was important, not only in formulating the problem and potential public awareness strategies, but also in making sure that the correct audience is targeted and that the appropriate message is framed for the audience. In a workshop summary for suicide prevention, for example, Chambers and associates (2005) found that working to focus the message to maintain the campaign's purpose was the most challenging part of public awareness strategies, but, if done correctly, it was also the most effective.

We have all seen billboards, public service announcements (PSAs), and other forms of public awareness campaigns where we wonder what the message is. In our policy practice class, for example, we spend time analyzing PSAs to assess quality in terms of the message, who we think they are trying to target, and so on. One, in particular, that troubles students is a 30-second message about the dangers of cocaine. After analyzing this message it becomes apparent that by showing someone actually using the drug, it may not only become normative, but for those who have had a problem with it in the past, watching someone "use" may not be the best way of trying to prevent it. Thus, as mentioned in Chapter 4, when using the media as a strategy it is important to analyze every aspect of a public service announcement to make sure the message is age appropriate, culturally (race, class, etc.) competent, targeted to a specific audience, and providing the intended message.

There are several intervention strategies that one can use in a community awareness project. Public service announcements are only one. Over the years, groups have used both general and targeted campaigns. General campaigns try to reach the largest audience, while targeted campaigns attempt to communicate the message to a specific sector of the population. Rapid Reference 7.1 shows different strategies that can be utilized for community awareness.

The first four strategies under general campaigns have been discussed at length in Chapter 4. Brochures and fliers can be used in general or targeted campaigns. They can be delivered to agencies, for example, that work with the population that you are trying to target. Information packets of resource material or public officials' e-mails and phone numbers can be put together for organizations, neighborhood canvassing, or to drop off at agencies that are willing to distribute them. Particularly for targeted mes-

≡ Rapid Reference 7.1

Community Awareness Strategies and Potential Target Populations

General Campaign	Targeted Campaign	Potential Target Populations
• Public service announcements • Letters to the editor • Op-eds • News release • Brochures • Fliers • Billboards	• Resource packets • Information booth • Forum • Curricula • Scorecards • Brochures • Fliers	• General population • Elderly • Health providers • Local business owners • Teens • Specific geographic communities • Populations sympathetic to a controversial issue

sages, it might be more appropriate to gather information and hold a forum or a meeting of like-minded individuals.

Here are some examples of targeted awareness campaigns, and the interventions decided upon by task groups:

- A task group wanted to create awareness among the elderly population of Pharmaceutical Patient Assistance programs. They used a targeted campaign, creating an easy-to-read, large-type brochure with information on how to access the program. They distributed these to places where they hoped to find the greatest proportion of elders: the local Office on Aging, retirement communities, and senior centers.
- The Teen Violence Task Force wanted to target teenagers for an awareness campaign on teen violence. They used a mixed ap-

proach, targeting both teens and the general public. Their interventions for the teen target included a PSA that focused targeted issues relevant to teenagers and a brochure distributed to local organizations and teen hangouts, such as the YWCA and the local shopping mall, that provided information on teen violence and where to go for help.

- A task group wanted to educate victims of stalking about their legal rights and methods of protection, as well as increase knowledge of existing resources in the community. The group used a mixed approach, targeting the general public, the university population, and specific locales where stalking victims might most likely come for help. They utilized the media by appearing on a local talk show on the public access channel, and developed information packets that they distributed to the domestic violence shelters, the victim's advocacy program, and the local university's women's center.

- Finally, an example of targeting populations sensitive to a controversial issue is the Youth Voice Task Force. This group worked on educating teenagers and progressive adults about potential changes in Title X funds for underage birth control users. The Parents' Right to Know Act, which was proposed in 2005, would have required minors to obtain written consent of a custodial parent in order to receive birth control, and the agencies providing birth control would lose Title X funds if they provided minors with birth control without permission from parents. Although the broad goal was to defeat the legislation, a targeted awareness campaign was utilized as one of the intervention strategies in order to inform affected parties of the bill's ramifications in order to get greater involvement to try to kill the bill. Of course, this bill would also have many supporters. So the task group targeted their interventions so that they would be able to reach people who opposed the legislation. First the group released a press release to publicize a health fair at a local high school. Notice they did not use the media to publicize the bill. They then distributed information regarding the upcoming legislation to teenagers, guidance counselors, and other like-minded people at the health fair. They also created and distributed a brochure to local organizations supporting youth's access to birth control that outlined the bill, gave information on where the bill was in the legislative process, and provided the names of the appropriate legislators to contact.

As you can see, project planning is crucial to the awareness campaign's success. The objectives flow from the goal, and the intervention strategies should be assessed to see if the correct population is being targeted and how best to reach that audience. The evaluation component in the planning process of awareness campaigns is important and should not be overlooked. How well the campaign was implemented, assessing whether the target population was reached, and analyzing what worked and didn't work, both in the framing of the message and in its delivery, are important information needed to either tweak the current information or learn important changes for future campaigns.

COMMUNITY-BASED POLICY PRACTICE AT THE LOCAL GOVERNMENT OR AGENCY LEVEL

So many local policies affect our lives and the lives of our clients. In social work, particularly, it is not uncommon to hear about policies that are having unintended negative consequences for our clients or in our neighborhood. It is often difficult to find out who is responsible for the policy, if it is even a formal policy (as opposed to an informal policy), what level of government has the authority to change the policy, and who to target to make the necessary changes. This is all before we even get to an intervention strategy, which is why the planning process outlined in Chapter 2 is so essential for community-based campaigns.

Over the last decade, I have witnessed task forces and coalitions change numerous policies at the local level. Often these policies are agency policies, so it requires a good analysis of the problem to ascertain at what level intervention should take place. Rapid Reference 7.2 lists a number of potential community-based project target systems and some of the areas where each of the targets have decision-making authority.

Local governments vary a great deal structurally, but each citizen has representation, just as at any other level of government. It is a good idea to get to know your local representative and attend a few council or commission meetings in order to understand how the process of local government works in your area. Bob Becker, a city council member in Knoxville, Tennessee, offered the following suggestions when working on local issues that the city council deals with directly, such as safety issues, development,

≡ *Rapid Reference 7.2*

Targets Systems for Change at the Local Level

- Local (city and county) government: responsible for local laws, oversees police and fire safety, public libraries, parks and recreation, and community development programs, including senior citizen centers, health, and housing developments. Also includes setting property tax rates, county health department, animal shelters, budgets for school boards, public housing authority
- Planning Commission: responsible for city- or county-wide planning, prepares and recommends zoning plans, urban redevelopment, transportation planning
- School board: develops and implements curriculum changes, develops zero-tolerance policies, sets school zone boundaries, renovates educational facilities
- Law enforcement agencies: crime prevention, first responders for domestic violence, orders of protection
- Local court system: child support enforcement, orders of protection
- Local housing authorities: zero-tolerance policies
- Transportation board: changes or additions to public transportation routes

zoning, and land use. First, he stressed that your councilperson is some-one from your neighborhood. Your children go to school together. You may attend the same church. People should feel comfortable calling and talking with them about issues. Some issues can be taken care of without a planned change strategy. For other, larger issues, he suggests that in-terested groups should come together and create a plan that outlines the problem or issue, alternative solutions to the problem, how much it would cost to fix the problem, and so on. By now the reader sees this as the first steps in the planning process from Chapter 2.

The next step is for your group to sit down with the council member from your district and ask him or her to support your plan. If the proposal is well thought out and straightforward, the council member may decide to sponsor the proposal or ordinance, and take it to the council meeting to present to the mayor and other members. The community group should attend this meeting in order to answer any questions. It is likely that the council will have to study the plan and bring it up again for vote after they have consulted relevant agencies and other constituents. An example that is occurring currently is the need for sidewalks in Becker's neighborhood. The neighborhood group that wants the sidewalks has approached Becker with their plan, and he has agreed to sponsor the ordinance and has taken it to council. The council asked the group to go to the city engineering department for more information on what it would take to provide side-walks in various areas of their neighborhood. There are several alternatives that may ultimately be chosen. Although the group would like the city to put in sidewalks in all of the proposed areas, depending on the budget, they may only be able to get incremental change. For example, one idea that has been proposed is that all new developments would be required to build sidewalks. Or, they may be able to get sidewalks in certain areas but not others. Remember that incremental change is a good beginning, so even though the overall goal may not be completely met, some change is better than no change, and there will be other times when the issue can be brought up again.

Although local government oversees school systems, law enforcement agencies, and other organizations listed in Rapid Reference 7.2, policy practice interventions targeting these agencies should first occur at the agency level, since they have their own policies and procedures that guide their organizations. School systems, for example, are often an important target. The school board, the local parent/teacher association (PTA), and even individual administrators, teachers, social workers, and guidance counselors can implement policies and, thus, are all potential targets for change.

Although it may seem that school systems are closed systems, meaning that they do not invite much participation, they are public entities and citizens have a right to become involved. Don't be put off if it seems difficult to access the school system; it may just take a bit of strategy to have your voice heard. A few years ago, when my daughter was in an elementary school in a large school district in the Midwest, the school opened up in the fall, but the library was not open. The school had moved to a larger building during the summer, but because of budget shortfalls there was only one librarian and she had no way of putting the library back together before the beginning of the school year. After a few discussions with the librarian and the principal on the timeline for the library to open, it was apparent that it could take months.

After some discussion with concerned neighbors, we decided to volunteer our time and come in shifts and help shelve all of the books. Much to our dismay the principal told us that the school board would not approve the offer because of liability issues. We held a community meeting and decided to approach the school board at their next meeting. But when we called to be put on the agenda, we were given mixed messages. Could we be put on the agenda? "Well, the agenda was pretty full . . ." What if we just showed up? "Well, it's a public meeting, I suppose you can show up; there is usually a community input section at the end of the agenda, but I can't guarantee . . ." and so on. Hmmm. We decided to go to the meeting. Our strategy was to bring all of our children with us. We thought that might be a good technique to get on the agenda, and it really was! The setup was a small room with a round boardroom table where all of the school board members sat. Around the side of the room there were chairs for the public (not many; I guess they didn't expect too many visitors). Eight parents were able to show up to the meeting. With them were a total of 10 kids, ranging from 2 to 10 years old. What a ruckus! Eighteen people stacked around the sides of the table. Needless to say, the community input part of the agenda was moved up to the front. We discussed the fact that we wanted to volunteer to put the library together. We presented two timelines: The first one showed how long the library would remain closed without volunteers; the second how much faster we could open it with volunteers. We also reminded the board that this was a public school and that parental involvement was important. The board voted unanimously to allow us to volunteer. The school library was open by the end of the month.

Rather than targeting the entire school board, other targets within the school system can be individual administrators and teachers. Each school has a certain amount of autonomy in the programs that they administer and implement. The Family Violence Task Force wanted to target teenagers by educating them about domestic violence and how to reduce the risk of youth becoming involved in abusive relationships. They first consulted with others who might be working on similar issues by contacting the family violence shelter in their area and the school social worker in the local high school. After looking at potential strategies, the task force decided to target one public high school that had an already established program that brought various social issues to the students through short-term seminars. Because the coordinator of the program was the vice principal of the school, the group was able to work with the administration to see what intervention strategies would work best to have the domestic violence issues introduced into the seminar. Working with the coordinator of the local family violence shelter, the group decided to create the curriculum for the school, complete with fact sheets, myths about violence and relationships, resource books, and quizzes for knowledge attainment.

They built relationships with the vice principal, the social worker, and the Family Violence Shelter staff. An unintended consequence was that these three stakeholders eventually built relationships among themselves, which made it more likely that this pilot project, if successful, might be implemented at more schools in the future. In the task force's evaluation of their successes and what they would do differently, they recognized that in future efforts working to network on a regular basis to have connections in the community prior to asking for help with a project would have been prudent, an insight that had been given by Becker, when he spoke of relationship building on a local level, and an insight that will be further explored in Chapter 8, working with the legislature at the state level.

Law enforcement is another example of an agency that can be targeted at the community level. For example, in Chapter 5 we were introduced to social workers in a domestic violence organization that realized that a rural law enforcement agency was having difficulty providing rapid assistance to domestic violence calls. Because of the large area that had to be covered (2,000 road miles) and inadequate resources to the county sheriff's department (the department could only respond to two calls at any given time), the department lacked personnel to respond to all domestic violence calls. This, coupled with a prevailing departmental attitude that the abused would not follow through with filing charges, that there was no shelter in the county, and no advocate in the county court system, created a situation where domestic violence calls were not seen as a priority in the county.

Although a new domestic violence law had been passed just 6 months earlier that required police to arrest the abuser, the abuser had to be present and evidence of the abuse obvious. The Domestic Violence Task Force met with the sheriff to discuss the barriers that the department faced, and he welcomed any assistance the task force could give to the department. After brainstorming potential interventions to assist in educating and assisting the police officers, taking the lack of resources into consideration, the task group came up with several tactics. First, they developed training materials in cooperation with experts in the field and educated the sheriff. Realizing that there was limited time and resources for in-service training with all of the officers, the task force targeted the sheriff so the sheriff could train others. They also developed the pocket card described in Chapter 5, so that police officers could have an easy resource to offer victims that included their rights, how to get orders of protection, and where they could go for safety.

The Domestic Violence Task Force was really surprised at how receptive the sheriff had been. But in a time of limited resources, and with the right set of interpersonal skills used by the task force, the sheriff saw the task force as a resource, not a threat. In fact, it was reported that after the training with the sheriff, he happened to attend a media event where he quoted several of the domestic violence statistics that had just been provided for him by the task force. These statistics were in turn published in a newspaper article covering the event. Hence, the group not only directly educated law enforcement, but was able to indirectly educate the public.

COMMUNITY-BASED INTERVENTION STRATEGIES

Attending Public Hearings and Public Meetings at the Local Level

If you decide that you would like to provide public testimony on an issue, you should first find out the specific protocol followed by the legislative body. Sometimes, members of the public can simply come to a local committee hearing or meeting, sign up at the door, and testify when their name is called. Usually, however, you must make arrangements to testify in advance with the committee staff. But it is much easier to gain access to local councils and boards than it is to testify before state or national legislative bodies.

When you decide to speak at a public hearing, there is great diversity in how this process works. The setup of the space is particularly important, because it sends a message to the speaker about how important her or his opinion is deemed by the representatives who originate the hearing. Sometimes the room is set up very formally, with the council or agency board in the front of the room, higher than the audience. As people speak, they may have to look up; they may be in the dark, while the members of the board are in a lighted area. It can be a bit intimidating, to say the least. If the board wants to send a particular message to the public, they may read the paper or talk to one another while people are testifying (I've actually had that happen to me). But you have a right to be heard, and some people are listening, especially the media, who generally show up for these events. On the other hand, I have been to some really good, democratic, open meetings where people's voices were very welcomed and decision makers really wanted and needed the feedback. And although the room may or may not be set up in a welcoming way, you can tell by the attitude of the hosts that your words are important to them and will be taken into consideration when they make their decision.

Public meetings are required for many projects that towns and cities want to undertake, from creating local hike and bike trails to developing a shopping mall. The hearings are designed to get community input and offer groups and individual citizens an opportunity to present their case to decision makers. Many agencies hold public meetings, including the parks and recreation commission, planning commission, city council, county commissions, and law enforcement agencies. It is very important to prepare ahead of time if the meeting is designed to make an immediate decision. You may have only one chance to give your arguments, so preparation is of the essence. Pick (1993) provides useful tips on how to prepare for a public meeting:

1. Maximize attendance: Spare no effort to notify as many concerned, like-minded people as possible of the meeting. If you have a task force or coalition already set up, or if you work with a community organization, send out a newsletter or postcard to your members.

2. Find out who will be present and who will speak. Generally, at a public meeting everyone who wants to speak can, but there are strict time limits, usually only about 5 minutes.

3. Prepare your speeches. Write down what you want to say. Prepare a document that combines all of the points to be given to the committee you are speaking to and to the press. Make sure everyone adheres to the time limit. Avoid too much repetition.

4. Agree to be respectful. Emotions may run high; there may be

opposition that has also organized against your position. Plan for this and remember, the calmer your group can stay, the more you will impress your opinion on the committee listening.

Although there are times when a public hearing is called to get the public's opinion on a matter, any time you want to talk to a government council or a public agency (school, housing authority, transportation board), remember that it is public. It is your right to be involved.

Working on Local Political Campaigns

One of the best ways to change policy at the local levels is to participate in, and/or run for, political office. Local grassroots political campaigns rely on volunteers to carry out their message and get people out to vote. Policy practitioners rely on local representatives to understand their position for change and to vote in their favor. It is a natural collaboration, then, for social workers to work with like-minded candidates to run for public office. First, I'll discuss briefly some important points to think about when deciding to run for office and provide a good reference for running a campaign at the local level. Then I will discuss some good grassroots campaign strategies that will be relevant, whether you are running for office or working on a candidate's campaign.

The first issue, of course, is deciding to run for office. It is generally friends and colleagues who encourage someone they know and think would be a good representative to run for a local office. If you are asked by friends and colleagues to run, think seriously about doing so. They obviously trust your judgment and believe that you (a) have a chance of getting elected, and (b) know the issues involved. Oftentimes the reason peers encourage you to run is based on your previous work in the community and how people view that work. It is important to think about whether this is something you want to do, how it will affect your family, whether it is the right timing personally, professionally, and politically, and if you feel you can make a difference by running.

Once you have made the decision to run, you will need to think about who can help you, who will be on your organizing committee. The people who asked you to run, of course, will be your first choice. But you also need to think about people close to you that may have expertise in raising money, budgeting, organizing volunteers, and running a campaign. *The Candidate's Handbook* (Yorke, 2003) outlines a series of questions that candidates should consider in the initial process of campaign development. These are:

- Why are you running?
- What are your qualifications?
- How much name recognition do you have?
- What are your bases of support?
- What are the issues and your positions on them?
- What kind of campaign do you plan?
- What will it cost?
- Do you have any personal problems that might interfere, from political problems to skeletons in the closet?
- You may also be asked about political ambitions, political philosophies, issues unrelated to the campaign, and any number of personal matters (p. 8).

Once these questions can be answered, it's time to write a personal fact sheet, a statement of your positions, estimate a tentative budget, and begin to list potential supporters and contributors to your campaign. One key to a good campaign (for any community-based intervention strategy) is to have a well-organized computer database of your potential and confirmed supporters. Gather information such as name, address, phone numbers, e-mail address, and voting precinct. Include database fields for each volunteer activity and record what each individual has volunteered to do. When it's time to contact supporters to door-knock, make phone calls, and so on, it's easy to pull up the list of willing volunteers from your database.

After an organizing committee is selected, the committee must work together to build a campaign organization. State and local campaigns differ, but all election campaigns thrive on organization and planning. So the

≣ *Rapid Reference 7.3*

The Planning Process in Local Election Campaigns

1. Set goals and define specific objectives.
2. Assemble facts necessary for the campaign and for your positions; study the issues.
3. Identify allies and opposition, pinpoint strengths and weaknesses.
4. Decide on your position and select strategies for campaign action.
5. List the materials and people needed to carry out campaign strategies.
6. Establish a timetable for completing each strategy.
7. Assign responsibilities for each action.
8. Budget: Determine how much each action will cost.

elements of the campaign plan are very important. Election laws differ across states and localities. Check with the election commission in your area before you start to plan the campaign.

Interestingly, the campaign planning strategy is very similar to our own planning process from Chapter 2. Rapid Reference 7.3 outlines the planning process of a political campaign. Notice the definition of goals and objectives, researching the issues, and planning intervention strategies. I would also strongly suggest using the strengths and weakness assessment for potential campaign strategies as well. Depending on the length of time of the campaign, the area in which you are in, and the issues of the campaign, some strategies will be better than others, and a thorough assessment of pros and cons of different campaign strategies is encouraged. The resulting campaign strategies should be designed to increase name recognition, raise money for the campaign, build a base of support, discuss issues, and persuade people to go the polls to vote for you.

Campaign Strategies

Web sites. With the proliferation of technology, depending on the size of your town, city, or county, a web site is a cost-effective way of utilizing your position paper and your candidate fact sheet to reach a large number of people. Web sites can also be used to raise awareness of issues and to invite people to volunteer on your campaign. A more in-depth discussion of the web as an overarching strategy for a variety of interventions is presented in Chapter 5, utilizing technology. For local elections, it is important to decide if a web site is needed in your campaign. How large is your district's constituency? Are voters in your district likely to view the web site? Do they have computers?

Canvassing neighborhoods. Another important strategy, particularly for local elections, is neighborhood canvassing, or "door knocking." Canvassing helps build name recognition, allows for a discussion of a candidate's position, and provides valuable information about the concerns of voters. It also provides an opportunity to obtain yard sign locations, which is a good way to locally advertise your candidacy. The following Putting It Into Practice illustrates how being able to talk to voters by going door to door can pave the way for greater support and, in this case, getting a yard sign put up to demonstrate that support.

It's important to target the households in a given neighborhood that are registered voters. The local registrar of elections can provide voter registration information, generally for a fee, that provides names, addresses, date of birth, declared party identification (in states where it is required), and the elections in which they voted. This can help focus your efforts on the most likely voters. As a volunteer, I have been given lists of voters in my neighborhood on a spreadsheet. I identify the most likely voters I will visit by how often they have voted in the last few years and in which party primary they typically vote. (Note: In Tennessee, voters do not register by party. They may choose the party primary they want to vote in for each election.) If time is limited, focus on older voters, since they are most likely to vote. It is important, particularly if volunteers are scarce, to have as much information as possible in order to make canvassing as efficient as possible.

Utilize the media. Extensive coverage of different media strategies is located in Chapter 4. This is a good time to use various media approaches

Putting It Into Practice

Canvassing Neighborhoods

When Madeline Rogero ran for mayor in 2003, door-knocking was an important part of her campaign strategy. When a voter showed any degree of interest, she always asked if she could put a campaign sign in the yard. Yard signs are a great strategy to generate awareness and demonstrate support. On one occasion, she knocked on the door of an elderly couple. The couple graciously invited her into the house and the husband said, "We think your opponent did a better job in the TV debate." "I don't think so," the wife replied softly. He continued, "We think your opponent is better prepared to be mayor." "I don't think so," the wife again said softly. "Well, we really haven't made up our minds," the husband said. "Oh, I have," said the wife softly but with conviction. With that, Madeline turned to the wife and, with a laugh, asked, "May I put a campaign sign in your half of the yard?" The wife looked at her husband. "Are you sure about this?" he asked. "Yes," she almost whispered. "Well, OK," he said, "put a sign in our yard."

to get your message and your candidacy out to the public. If you are on a tight budget, use letter writing, press releases, community calendars of upcoming events, and opinion pieces to get the word out.

Seek support. It is a good idea to talk to as many groups as possible in your voting district, particularly if they are likely to be friendly constituents. If you are a member of a church, a local charity club or political organization, a member of a homeowners association, or have children in school, you have a natural group of individuals and friends to ask to support your campaign. The National Association for Social Workers (NASW) endorses candidates for election through their local PACE (political action for candidate endorsement) committees. Some NASW PACE committees only endorse candidates at the state level, but others endorse local campaigns as well. At the least, contact them to let them know to put your candidacy in the next issue of the newsletter to increase your name recognition and let other members read about your position.

Putting It Into Practice

The Case for Human Billboarding

Madeline Rogero won a successful bid for county commission in 1990, defeating a 24-year incumbent. One of her favorite campaign strategies was human billboarding with a big group of supporters and her family at a busy intersection in her district during the week before the election. Every morning, they held signs that said "Vote for Madeline" and "Honk for Madeline." Her 11- and 14-year old children held "Vote for My Mom" signs, and even her mother was there with a sign that said, yes, "Vote for my Daughter." They made sure to make eye contact with drivers and to smile and wave. The recognition and response built day by day until, on election day, drivers were looking for them, honking, giving the thumbs-up sign, and some even yelled out "I'm votin' for ya!" On the day after Madeline's landslide victory, they were back out with "Thank you" signs. One gentleman stopped his car, got out and walked up to Madeline. He said, "My wife and I have been watching you out here every day. We got up this morning and my wife said 'I wonder if she'll be out there this morning.'" He leaned closer. "Honey," he said, "This will get you re-elected!" During her 4-year term, countless individuals commented favorably to Madeline that they had seen her human billboarding. And, by the way, she did get re-elected.

Human billboarding. I haven't seen this mentioned in the literature I've read on local grassroots campaigns, but it is a strategy that I have seen work with success at the local level. The Putting It Into Practice above provides an example of the successful use of human billboarding. Human billboards are a strategy where candidates and/or volunteers locate themselves at busy intersections or business areas with signs that ask voters to vote for them or, if volunteering, their candidate. It is a creative way to remind people to vote, particularly if used just a few days before the election.

Whether you are planning to run for election or volunteer for a campaign, these tactics should prove useful. There are plenty of other strategies that can be used for grassroots elections, some more successful than others, and this will depend largely on the area where you live. There are several books available on running for grassroots elections, but the one I found particularly useful, which I cited previously, is *The Candidate's Handbook for Winning State and Local Elections* by Harvey Yorke.

SUMMARY

Several lessons learned in this chapter are worth reiterating here. Building relationships with leaders, administrators, and agency personnel prior to planning a change project are very important. It saves a lot of time to already have relationships and networks built in the community before an issue arises. This may seem like a lofty goal, but every social worker already works in a specific area of expertise; thus, there are coalitions, community organizations, and other opportunities to become involved, so that your name is recognized as a resource prior to initiating a project. Likewise, attending community meetings of interest is another way to stay informed of the issues and to meet people in the community who may become a resource later on. Being involved in the community, in your school, and in local issues affecting your neighborhood are all ways to establish credibility. Remember, however, that because some issues may become highly charged, using your interpersonal social work skills will create and maintain your reputation as a thoughtful and valuable colleague and member of your community.

 **TEST YOURSELF**

Break into groups, and using the planning process from Chapter 2, develop a plan for one of the following:

A. As a school social worker, you are concerned about domestic violence in the teenagers' relationships at your school. You would like to bring awareness to this issue and also provide education and resources where teens can go for help if there is a problem. What kind of an awareness campaign would you want to create? What steps would need to be taken for this to be successful?

(continued)

B. You are a hospital social worker. You are worried about some of the new mothers that are leaving the hospital with their newborns, who are exhibiting early signs of post-partum depression. But there is no follow-up program for this potential problem at the hospital. Although there are resources in the community, there is no coordination between the programs and no outreach to new mothers. What can be done?

Using the planning process, answer the following questions.

1. Describe the problem.

2. Analyze the problem and the policy change needed.

3. Design a broad goal.

4. Derive measurable objectives to meet the goal.

5. Brainstorm possible strategies and tactics to meet the objectives.

6. Assess the advantages and disadvantages for each possible strategy.

7. Choose the best tactics with the least obstacles.

8. Provide a rationale for your choices.

9. Provide a plan to evaluate your progress toward your goal.

Eight

ESSENTIALS OF LEGISLATIVE POLICY PRACTICE

T his chapter focuses on the legislative process and how social workers can intervene at this level. This chapter relates to the state and federal level, since local level political systems were discussed in depth in Chapter 7. Because we are geographically closer to our state legislators, there are many opportunities to build relationships, communicate, and lobby at this level. It is at this level that I will focus, but these techniques can work at the federal level as well. However, given the current political climate, a great proportion of decision making is also being handed down to the state level; thus, it is an important area to target.

The chapter is outlined as follows. First, a brief overview of the legislative process and the importance of the committee system of government is given. Next, how the legislative process can be influenced and what is considered lobbying from a legal standpoint is discussed. Most people, social workers included, have been given a very broad definition of lobbying, and there is trepidation in the field as to what we can and cannot do as citizens and professionals in performing policy practice tasks. Social workers can perform many policy practice activities without surpassing the legal definition of being a lobbyist, and this will be discussed in some depth. After we have a good understanding of where our boundaries for lobbying are, the following section provides intervention strategies for targeting legislators for change. Effective change strategies at the state and national level are discussed, including how to influence legislators without being a paid lobbyist, how to work with lobbyists, how to introduce a bill, and how to kill a bill in committee. Putting It Into Practice vignettes will be used in this chapter to show how grassroots efforts of social workers have made a difference in real ways at the state level. The importance of becoming involved in organizations that have political action committees, paid lobbyists, and legislative committees is also discussed. Political Action Committees (PACs) are designed to endorse candidates for elections, a very important task that 501(c)(3) nonprofit organizations are absolutely forbidden from doing. Political Action Committees will be discussed both in terms of their importance, their limitations, and how social workers can utilize existing PACs without losing their 501(c)(3) status.

FEDERAL AND STATE LEGISLATIVE PROCESS

Most policy in the United States is decided in both federal and state legislatures. While much attention is given to the federal government and the laws that are created at that level, the last 3 decades have seen major reductions in federal influence in social legislation. Instead, states have taken over much of the responsibility in both policy creation and implementation of policies and programs. Devolution, as discussed earlier, has decentralized governmental responsibility of policy down to the state level. And while broad policy may be created at the federal level, state governments have been given authority in how to shape and pay for social welfare services.

The legislative process of federal and state government policymaking is largely the same. Rapid Reference 8.1 illustrates the policymaking process at both the federal and state levels. Both state and federal governments have two chambers, the House and Senate (except for Nebraska, which only has a senate). The committee process by which bills are debated is similar to the federal government, and the mechanisms for signing a bill into law by the executive branch are also the same. Therefore, the discussion of the process of legislative policymaking will be the same for both the federal and state level.

Lobbyists and policy advocates are working at every stage of the process if they are tracking a piece of legislation that they want passed (or

≡ Rapid Reference 8.1

The Policymaking Process at the Federal and State Legislative Level (Note: Nebraska will only have the senate version of this chart)

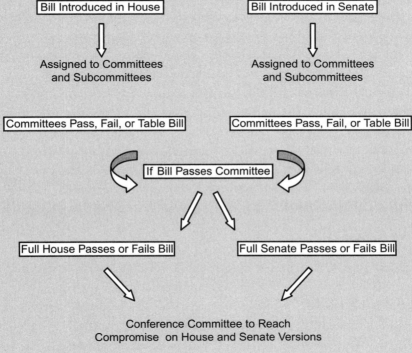

Bill Introduced in House

⬇

Assigned to Committees and Subcommittees

Committees Pass, Fail, or Table Bill

If Bill Passes Committee

Full House Passes or Fails Bill

Bill Introduced in Senate

⬇

Assigned to Committees and Subcommittees

Committees Pass, Fail, or Table Bill

Full Senate Passes or Fails Bill

Conference Committee to Reach Compromise on House and Senate Versions

House Passes Compromise

Senate Passes Compromise

President or Governor

Signs, Takes No Action, or Vetoes Bill

defeated). Each committee that their bill goes through requires a concerted effort by policy practitioners to contact members of that committee to explain the merits of their bill. Much work goes into gaining support for a bill, long before it is even introduced; finding sponsors, seeking support from coalitions, finding out who may decide to come out against the bill, and looking for compromises.

As Rapid Reference 8.1 indicates, bills are introduced in each of the houses separately. Each bill goes through various committees for debate, and on to specific subcommittees as needed. Amendments can be attached to the bills at either of these levels. Committees and subcommittees can stop a bill by voting against it or tabling the bill and not acting on it. It is actually much easier to kill a bill than it is to pass it. While legislators deal with thousands of bills each session, only a small portion of those ever make it to the House or Senate floor to be voted on. If a bill does make it out of committee it is likely that it will pass the full House or Senate. However, the president (or governor, at the state level) can still kill a bill by veto, unless the legislature can muster a two-thirds majority to override it.

Committees

Groups seeking to pass or defeat legislation may feel overwhelmed by the task of convincing the whole state legislature of their position. But because it is a committee system, groups should spend time working on a bill, committee by committee. Persons learning about the legislative process are often surprised to learn how crucial committees are. The main reason is that no bill can progress to the next committee or to the whole body (the floor) until it is recommended by the committee(s) to which it is assigned. The Speaker assigns each bill to a standing committee based on its subject matter. Depending on the state you are in, the House (or General Assembly) and Senate may make use of subcommittees. In Tennessee, the House committee chairs assign bills to subcommittees. The Senate has traditionally not had many subcommittees. A bill must get a majority of the committee members' votes or it is dead or stalled. Committees do not simply advise the full House and Senate. Their votes control whether the legislation ever makes it to the floor in most states.

In each of these committees and subcommittees, the bill sponsor is present to speak for and explain the implications of the bill. In most states, the bulk of discussion and amendment of bills takes place in these committees, not on the House and Senate floor. At the request of a committee member or the bill's sponsor, a nonlegislator may be asked to address the committee on the bill.

All committee meetings are open for the public to attend, but are not public hearings in that nonlegislators do not have the right to speak, as is the case with local government. Citizens and lobbyists are not given the opportunity to speak unless the sponsor or a committee member requests it. Normally, this is worked out beforehand with the committee chair. Thus, it is important to know which legislators are on which committees when following a piece of legislation. If you are a resource for that legislator, you have a greater likelihood of being asked to testify before the committee. Interestingly, if you are a resource to a lobbyist who is a resource to the committee, you may also be asked to testify. That was my experience several years ago, when I was asked to testify before the TennCare Oversight Committee because I had done research that a pharmaceutical lobby found beneficial to their position (see Chapter 6, Putting It Into Practice vignette "Strange Bedfellows in the Policy Process").

While it is not easy to pass a bill, it is not impossible. Remember these concrete steps and opportunities:

- Provide the sponsor with good information and fact sheets.
- Be at committee meetings to speak as a resource if asked (and arrange to be asked beforehand if you and the sponsor think it advisable).
- Focus advocacy on the committee, not the whole legislative body, until the bill gets past committee; then broaden the targets.

These steps are important in defeating bills as well as passing them. However, the burden of passing a bill is on supporters, not opponents.

While we may not be able to testify, we can speak with committee members about the bill before it comes before the committee. If a committee member is from your district, then hopefully you will already have a relationship with this person.

Introducing Legislation

If your group wants to introduce legislation, the process of tracking the legislation and educating legislators, particularly committee members, is similar to that described previously, but introducing legislation starts much earlier, and it is a process that requires a great deal of planning before the legislature convenes for the session. When a membership organization wants to introduce legislation it requires a great deal of planning up front by the legislative committee. Rapid Reference 8.2 provides a checklist for introducing legislation.

Sponsors are very important. Not only do you want bipartisan sponsorship, for obvious reasons, but the right sponsors are also important. Look at who the party leaders are and who chairs the committees that the bill

Rapid Reference 8.2

Tips for Introducing Legislation

- Start early, well before the legislative session begins.
- Plan ahead for the right sponsors.
- Get bipartisan support.
- Obtain the support of the governor and relevant state agencies.
- Introduce the bill as early as possible.
- Provide sponsor with accurate information.
- Track the legislation as it moves through committee.
- Be a resource.
- Be prepared for incremental change; amend the bill, if necessary.

will likely go through. If at all possible, sponsors should be seasoned legislators on good committees. A sponsor who is new or not that interested in the bill can do more harm than good. All potential stakeholders must be identified and assessed to see whether they will support or oppose the bill. Because the legislative process centers largely around compromise, it is important to know if there will be groups that may oppose your bill and try to work out differences beforehand.

The Putting It Into Practice on page 132 provides an example of a bill that went before the Tennessee Legislature in 2005 that provided title protection for social workers. Although it passed, there were numerous decisions and compromises that had to be made along the way.

The Social Work Consumer and Title Protection Act is a good example of the type of incremental change that is typical in getting a bill passed. Had we held out for the entire state to be protected, we probably could not have gotten the bill passed. Now a large percentage of social workers are protected. We can attempt to look into the nursing home situation at another time, when there is more time to examine it, or we can try to get the national NASW legislative committee to work on it at the federal level.

The legislative committee also made sure that the membership was given talking points when they called from their home towns to support the legislation. It was important to ensure that consumer protection was used, because it isn't just social workers who will be protected. Finally, it was important to push through the legislation as quickly as possible—in this case, because of other agendas that might not have proved favorable to our cause if it had gone through later. This is one example of how much strategy must go into the decisionmaking process when introducing legislation.

LOBBYING: WHAT IT IS AND WHAT IT ISN'T

Lobbying and 501(c)(3) Nonprofit Organizations

According to Raffa (2000), many nonprofit 501(c)(3) organizations misunderstand what they can and cannot do to influence the public policy

Putting It Into Practice

Social Work Consumer and Title Protection Act

In 2005, the Tennessee chapter of NASW introduced a bill to protect the title of social workers. In the proposed legislation only social workers with an MSW or a BSW could use the title *social worker*. It would seem that this would be a pretty straightforward process. Nurses cannot call themselves nurses, for example, unless they have an RN or LPN license. But it was not as simple as it appeared. It was political and required a great deal of strategy to get it passed. Everything was important to take into consideration, from the name of the bill, who might support or oppose it, how fast we should try to get the legislation introduced and acted upon (depending on what other issues we were working on), and what amendments might need to be considered.

First, the name was important. We wanted to make sure that legislators understood that protecting the title of social worker helped protect consumers of social services, not just the social work profession. Next, the committee scanned various agencies and organizations to see who might support or oppose the bill. Another decision that had to be made was when to introduce the bill and who would be good sponsors. It was decided to introduce the bill as early in the legislative session as possible, for two reasons. First, it would give less time for potential opposition to mobilize, and the legislation's early passage would allow NASW to dedicate additional attention later to other issues. We attempted to find sponsors from both parties and from members from key committees that we knew the bill would have to pass through.

As the NASW legislative committee followed the bill through committees, they e-mailed the membership with alerts to contact various legislators at strategic points. An oversight in the scan process was encountered when the nursing home association objected to the legislation, as there was a federal regulation related to nursing homes that defined social workers differently. The TN-NASW had to decide whether to accept an amendment that would allow persons to practice as social workers in nursing homes under the federal definition. Given that the development of legislation often requires compromise and that we would be opposed by a strong nursing home lobby, we decided to amend the bill to allow persons to practice in nursing homes based upon the federal regulation. The amendment was added to the bill to avoid any controversy that could have delayed or killed the bill in committee, and the legislation was ultimately passed.

After the bill was passed into law, one metropolitan agency realized it would have to change some social worker job titles to comply with the law and has vowed to try to amend the legislation in the next session. The executive director of the NASW chapter is now trying to work out these issues, but it is still unknown if we will be facing additional amendments in the next legislative session.

arena. First and foremost, an individual can lobby as often as she or he chooses. Acting as an individual constituent and not part of an organization has its pluses and minuses. On the plus side, one is not constrained by the lobbying laws regarding charitable organizations. On the negative side, it is a good idea to be part of a larger organization. But individual constituents do have substantial influence over public officials, and if they have established themselves as an expert in their field (outside of their organization, of course) they can become an important source of information for their legislators.

The second misunderstanding that many nonprofits have is that the tax code defines *advocacy* activities differently than it defines *lobbying.* The tax code defines lobbying as an attempt by an organization to influence a specific piece of legislation, and/or to attempt to influence the public on a specific piece of legislation. There are no laws governing how an organization advocates on behalf of its clients or communities. Advocacy can encompass many activities for organizations, including efforts to influence administrative agencies to change policies, rules, or regulations (which will be discussed in more detail in Chapter 9), developing policy positions directed at issues that are not specifically designated toward a specific piece of legislation, testifying before legislative committees, voter registration drives, nonpartisan voter education material, and providing research and other information to legislators. All of these activities can be done by organizations without any worries about lobbying protocol.

If your organization wants to become more active in supporting or opposing specific pieces of legislation, they can—within certain parameters. According to the tax laws, a tax-exempt nonprofit organization can lobby as long as it is not a "substantial" part of their organizational activity. Raffa (2000) says the traditional test for "substantial" is less than 5 percent of an organization's activities. But there are several options that organizations can use if they want to lobby specific pieces of legislation more substantially. First, organizations can employ Section 501(h) of the tax code, which states that a public charity can spend up to a certain dollar amount of its exempt expenditures to influence legislation without incurring a tax or losing its exempt status. For an organization that has tax-exempt expenditures of $500,000 or less, they may spend up to 25 percent of their expenditures on lobbying. If an organization spends in excess of the amounts allocated under Section 501(h), it will owe a 25 percent tax on its lobbying expenses. It is important to note that organizations should not do this for more than a couple of years, because if it occurs for more than 4 years, the organization can lose its nonprofit status.

If your organization plans on spending more than 25 percent of its expenditures on lobbying it may be a good idea to establish a 501(c)(4) organization. This is a sister organization to your 501(c)(3) organization, meaning that you can have both simultaneously. Your organization is still tax exempt, but people who contribute are not eligible for the charitable deduction afforded to the contributors of a 501(c)(3). As long as your (c)(4) organization does not receive any money from its sister organization, then there are no restrictions on lobbying at all. Many community organizations choose to have both statuses, since often part of their mission is to influence the legislative arena.

The Hatch Act and Its Implications for Lobbying

The Hatch Act was passed in 1939 to limit the political activities of federal and some state executive branch employees. The act is mostly concerned with partisan political activities, meaning those activities which help people get elected. Unfortunately, the Act has been interpreted to mean that all political activities by government employees are banned. This is simply not true; the Act is primarily concerned with partisan politics. Rapid Reference 8.3 distinguishes between activities that are permitted and prohibited by the Hatch Act (Haynes & Mickelson, 2003).

What becomes fairly obvious when looking at permitted and prohibited activities is that the law is aimed not at being politically active, or advocating for certain legislation, but at working on election campaigns to have certain candidates, or parties, elected. Unfortunately, this Act has been used to keep social workers in state and federal agencies from advocating at the legislative level. I have had social workers tell me that their agencies have told them it is illegal for them to even write letters as citizens advocating for policies to assist their clients. While I'm sure there is a certain

≡ *Rapid Reference 8.3*

Activities Permitted and Prohibited for Government Employees

Permitted Activities

- Register to vote and vote
- Express political views publicly and privately
- Participate in nonpartisan campaigns
- Assist in voter registration activities
- Contribute to political organizations
- Wear political buttons off duty
- Run in nonpartisan elections
- Lobby for or against referendums, constitutional amendments, and local ordinances

Prohibited Activities

- Run for or hold partisan political office
- Distribute campaign literature in partisan elections
- Endorse candidates in partisan elections
- Solicit contributions or organize partisan fundraisers

amount of fear associated with crossing the line politically for executive agencies, it is important to know the law. How can we possibly help our clients if we are never allowed to tell anyone what is happening to them?

CHANGE STRATEGIES AT THE LEGISLATIVE LEVEL

When we think of lobbyists, we often think of people who work full time for powerful corporations such as the tobacco industry or insurance companies. Although this is certainly true, much lobbying also takes place by individuals who are constituents of the representative they are speaking with, or individuals who represent smaller coalitions of grassroots interest groups. A good lobbyist provides scientific, unbiased information in a simple-to-understand presentation to her or his representatives while she or he discusses the importance of their position. Lobbyists have good interpersonal skills and maintain relationships with legislators by providing information on relevant topics.

I have often been told by state legislators that lobbyists are important to legislators. They provide more information for decision making than any other source they have. Especially at the state level, where legislators do not have the budgets to hire many administrative and research assistants, they rely on the information brought to them by lobbyists. Furthermore, state legislators have told me many times over the years that few constituents contact them about specific pieces of legislation unless it is a very hot topic. Given that thousands of bills are introduced each legislative session, it is no wonder that legislators rely on lobbyists.

Information is definitely an important commodity that legislators need. My students and I had an interesting experience with a legislator who we were actually just visiting for educational purposes. An upcoming subcommittee vote was weighing heavily on his mind. He began talking about the vote and asked the students, as social workers, what they thought. It was obvious that he had not made up his mind on the issue. They began to discuss the issue, the pros and cons, how it might affect the community. We had actually already discussed the bill as a group before meeting with the representative. So when the legislator brought it up, it was an opportunity to provide some information. We decided to go to the committee hearing the following day. This particular legislator ended up voting the way that we had hoped and even used some of the students' language when he stated his opinion during the committee hearing.

This incident illustrates just how important it is for social workers to provide education from our clients' perspective. Without it, it is difficult for people to understand their reality, to be able to step into another's environment to see what may best assist them.

Community-Based Policy Practice Targeting the State or National Level

Hearing from constituents back home is a powerful message for legislators. As we just discussed, legislators often receive the bulk of their information by which they make decisions from lobbyists and interest group organizations. But citizens from their voting districts are important to them. As we saw in Chapter 3, one reason why it took so long to pass the Family Medical Leave Act was the lack of grassroots support. Targeting legislation at any level of government from the ground up can be very effective. Here are some community-based intervention strategies with examples targeting different levels of government or bureaucratic agencies.

Communicating with Your Representatives
Writing letters, calling representatives on the phone, and visiting them one on one are important parts of political participation. They know how lobbyists feel, but if they hear the opposite from their hometown it makes a difference.

Letter-writing campaigns. A personal letter from a constituent is a very powerful advocacy tool. In general, an effective letter is limited to one or two pages at the most. Start and end your letter by stating why you are writing and what it is you would like your representative to do. The tone of your letter should always be professional and courteous, even when you disagree with someone's position, or are expressing disappointment about an action he or she took. Good use of interpersonal skills is important, even in letter writing. Although there are many opportunities to send form letters to candidates (e.g., letters from Web-based groups, as described in Chapter 5), a personalized letter is always best. Even if you do belong to a listserv and have form letters ready to send from the computer, it is best to change the format and content a bit to personalize the letter.

There are certain ways to write a letter that will receive more attention than others. Generally the least effective method, as mentioned previously, are form letters. These letters all say the same thing and all people do is sign their name and send them in. Once a representative notices that form letters are being sent in, it works much like a petition. They keep track of how many they receive, but your individual story remains untold. The best letter is the one that you sit down and write yourself.

A well-written personal letter may be the most effective way to communicate your message. All elected officials want to know how people feel about issues. A good letter contains four important components:

- First, you should summarize your position on the issue.
- Second, let the representative know how this issue is affecting you or will affect you personally.
- Third, let him or her know of others who will be affected.
- Fourth, describe what action you think the representative needs to take.

It is also a good idea to acknowledge that the representative has made the right decisions in the past and that you are counting on him or her to do the same in this instance.

Don't be surprised or disappointed if you receive a form letter in return, particularly at the federal level. But don't think your letter doesn't count; at the federal level they keep a tabulation of opinion, and letters are one way to convey that opinion. At the state level, letters are much more likely to be read and answered personally. In my conversations with lawmakers, I have been surprised to hear more than once that two or three good letters from home made the difference in how they voted on an issue. Letters from their constituents mean a great deal to them and may help them make their decision.

Phone calls and e-mail. Making phone calls and e-mailing are other ways to get your message to representatives. You shouldn't, however, expect to get your legislator on the phone, especially at the state or federal level. Generally, if it is a big political issue, an aide is assigned to answer phone calls and write down what constituents say. They will ask your name, address (make sure you are in their district), and whether you support the proposed bill. It usually isn't a good idea to make a long statement if you are talking to an aide. They may or may not know what the issues are, and are only instructed to take down minimal information. Do be sure to have the bill number and name handy when you call. Although it may seem like they didn't take much information down, they are keeping a running tab of what people want and it will be passed on. Phone calls count, and two or three phone calls can make a difference.

E-mail addresses are now provided for most elected officials. They are generally answered by an aide at the federal level, but as with phone calls and letters, your responses are noted. At the state level, my experience has been that legislators generally respond to their own e-mails, unless they feel the e-mails are part of a concerted effort, or a form letter. Ways to get around having your e-mail appear to be a form letter are discussed in depth in Chapter 5. If you are unsure of your legislator's contact information, or even who your legislators are at various levels of government, refer to Rapid Reference 5.5, which provides two web sites you can use to find out who represents you at the federal, state, and local levels.

Personal visits. Personal visits to your representatives are an ideal way to build positive relationships with representatives, especially at the state and local levels. Make an appointment before you drop by. If you are interested in a bill, bring the bill number and name with a brief description of your position as their constituent, or your organization's position if you are representing an agency, to leave with them when you leave. Do a bit of homework before the visit. Know your representatives, where they live, what school they went to, what organizations they belong to, where they work. Building relationships is very important in politics, and finding common ground before your visit can make a difference. One last tip: Never threaten an elected official with innuendo or direct comments about not voting for them in the next election if they do not vote for your bill. All of the legislators that I have spoken with take those comments very negatively on a personal level. Don't burn bridges. While a legislator may vote against your position on one issue, she or he may support your position on another. Therefore, good interpersonal relationships cannot be overstated.

Stewart Clifton, a lobbyist for NASW, Tennessee chapter, was kind enough to provide tips for citizens who want to have an effective visit with their legislator. Rapid Reference 8.4 presents Clifton's tips for communicating with legislators in person.

Testifying before Committees

For legislative testimony it is important to present yourself either as an expert in the field or as part of a larger advocacy effort. Presenting on the part of a professional association claims expertise as well as being a constituent. Ineffective testimony will undermine the cause and can damage future efforts of the advocate or organization (Richan, 1996). Therefore, it is important to demonstrate both confidence and integrity. Rapid Reference 8.5 provides some important tips when testifying before legislative committees.

Anticipate arguments that may be given during a question-and-answer period, never lose your composure, and never try to make jokes during the presentation. Others may not have the same sense of humor as you. Usually the press will be present for committee hearings. It is wise to have a smaller fact sheet with you to hand out to the press, with your important points highlighted (Sharwell, 1982). This makes it easier for reporters to pick up the important points of the presentation.

≡ Rapid Reference 8.4

Lucky 13 Tips for In-Person Visits with Elected Officials

1. Make appointments beforehand if possible. Otherwise drop by and inquire of staffer if this is a possible time for a visit.

2. Sometimes meeting with a key staffer is almost as good as meeting with a legislator. Don't turn that down if offered, unless you are sure you can get to see the elected official.

3. Be courteous but don't apologize. You have a right to try to influence your elected officials, to meet with them, and to express your views.

4. Remember you are building a relationship. Unless you really are a close friend, introduce yourself and wear a name tag, and when possible, a group identification.

5. If you already know the elected officials or at least have met them, make sure you tell them and remind them of how you know them.

6. Tell them if you are a constituent.

7. Appoint a key spokesperson if in a group, but introduce everyone.

8. Provide short, clear information—no jargon! Best points only, written and oral.

9. Don't overstay.

10. Don't threaten or otherwise burn bridges.

11. Ask for a vote for your position and try to get an answer. But remember, it's legitimate for elected officials to reserve judgment on a bill.

12. Thank them for meeting with you and follow oral thanks with a written note.

13. Follow up as needed. When you leave the meeting, your work is often just beginning. Arrange for the legislator's questions to be addressed and for others to contact.

≡ Rapid Reference 8.5

Tips on How to Successfully Testify before Legislative Committees

The Substance of the Testimony

- Be aware of the issues—express ideas and issues clearly and succinctly.
- Be aware of alternatives to your argument and be able to state why your proposal is better than alternative suggestions.
- Be able to state specifically the route that the legislation should take.
- Accurately and fully disclose all information.
- Never mislead the committee, because if there is a flaw in your argument, your opponents will bring it out if you do not.

The Structure of the Testimony

- Make a short introductory statement, who you are, and who you represent.
- The body of the testimony should include your argument (the rationale, based on research or law).
- A story can be worth a thousand statistics. Use both.
- Be prepared to refute counterarguments.
- Use short closing remarks, again thanking the committee and providing contact information for further questions.
- Have copies of your testimony for all members and the press.

THE PLANNING PROCESS AT THE LEGISLATIVE LEVEL

Since we do not want to divorce the planning process from all of the above-mentioned strategies, it is a good idea to revisit the planning stages that must go into a change strategy at the legislative level. The following Putting It Into Practice provides an illustration of a task force that worked to amend the state's spousal rape laws, and provides an example of how they planned out their strategies to target the state legislature.

The task force maintained contact with the sponsors of the bill and

Putting It Into Practice

Grassroots Change Strategy at the State Level

The Spousal Rape Law Task Force had seven members, two men and five women, all masters-level social work students, most of whom were currently working as social workers in the field. They were a grassroots task force, located 2½ hours from the state capitol.

Problem Identification: There was a bill introduced in the legislature that would amend the then-current Spousal Rape Law to remove certain exclusions in the law that would strengthen its protection for spouses raped by their partners.

Target System and Others Working on the Issue: The target system was the state legislature. The task force found two other organizations that were working on the same issue, and collaborated with them to find effective strategies and avoid duplication of their efforts.

The Goal: The goal was to amend the state's spousal rape law—to remove exclusions and strengthen the law.

Objectives: They devised two objectives: (1) To educate and lobby their representatives to support the bill, and (2) to garner community support for the legislation.

Action Strategies: After some discussion of alternative strategies that the group could use, they decided on a multipronged approach. Given that they were miles away from the capitol, intense lobbying on the hill was out of the question; the other two organizations working on the bill would have to take that task. There was a Domestic Violence Lobbying Day coming up, but only one of the group's members could attend. Therefore, they decided to use a grassroots effort and utilized the following tactics: To address objective 1, they each wrote letters to all of their state representatives, they wrote letters to the editors and sent them to five newspapers, one member went to the capitol for the lobbying day, and they tracked the legislation through committees, keeping track of any issues that arose. To address objective 2, they e-mailed friends and colleagues to ask them to support the bill by contacting their legislators, and created brochures and distributed them to all local organizations that they felt might support the legislation.

tracked its movement through the House and Senate. To their surprise, the bill became hotly contested in the House. At one point it looked like the bill would not pass, when it was referred to the budget subcommittee in the House (also known as the "dead" committee, since bills often die there). But they continued contacting legislators, talking about the importance of the bill, providing information. They targeted one of the House members who opposed the bill to try to influence him to change his mind. They wrote letters explaining the importance of the bill and told stories of victims who this bill could have helped. Much to the surprise of the task force, the representative that opposed the bill actually called both of the male members of the task force to ask why they were supporting it (much to the chagrin of the women). One of the men had a 45-minute conversation with him on the merits of the bill over the phone. At the end of the semester, the bill had made it out of the budget subcommittee and was in the judicial committee. It looked as if it would pass, but the task force concluded without knowing the end result.

In June, I received a letter from one of the task force members. He wrote, "I just received the attached letter. It is gratifying to know that our project may have been instrumental in this legislation successfully passing through the state legislature." The letter he attached was from his state representative and it read, "As you may already know, the bill passed the Senate and the House with no dissenting votes and should have been signed by the Governor by the time you receive this letter." Two important points should be made here. First, no dissenting votes meant that they really did change the mind of the one representative who was opposing the passage of that bill. Second, at the beginning of the semester I had one student who came into my course with the firm conviction that a small group of social workers could not make a difference at the legislative level, particularly when they were so far removed geographically from the legislature. Ironically, he was one of the members of this task force. He was also one of the men who was called on the phone by his representative. When that legislation passed, he told me with a smile, "Okay, you've convinced me! We really can make a difference."

I don't want to make it sound like every time we try to make a change we are successful. I would say that out of the projects that are done each semester, maybe half are successful. But at least another 25 percent have set the stage for future efforts. In a recent, unsuccessful bid to pass a law requiring emergency contraception to be offered at all emergency rooms for victims of sexual assault, a student came to me and said, "A lobbyist told me that even though our bill was killed, they are going to use our research to introduce another bill next session that has a better chance of passing." Legislative policy practice is slow, and there are political windows that open and close. And when legislation does get passed, it is often incremental, meaning you don't get everything that you wished for. But the payoffs, when they come, are important. Just understand that change takes time, patience, and perseverance.

INTEREST GROUP POLITICS REVISITED

It is worth reiterating that being part of a larger group of like-minded people is important at the state and federal legislative levels. Member organizations, such as NASW, are vital in being able to stay informed on important issues that affect you, your job, your clients, and the community. We discuss membership organizations and interest group politics in Chapter 6 in terms of coalitions and task forces that work on policy issues. Another set of interest groups that are important are legislative committees of member organizations and political action committees (PACs).

Legislative Committees

The legislative process works entirely around compromise. Committees are much more likely to support a bill if there is little controversy surrounding it. Conversely, a bill is much more likely to die in committee if it is steeped in controversy. Working with legislative committees of membership organizations is an important way to keep a large body of constituents knowledgeable about upcoming legislation, as well as to track legislation for members to act on when it comes to specific committees. Chapter 5 discussed the various ways to stay informed about legislation in your area of interest by using the Internet. Member organizations that have legislative committees are one example of organizations that use the Internet to organize grassroots constituents around policy issues. Technology has become an important way to be active in a timely manner when issues of interest arise. When there are bills that come up that interest their membership, legislative committees can easily contact a large number of people who will act on the legislation, either supporting it or opposing it. The NASW, for instance, sends out legislative alerts by e-mail that provide information on what committee a priority bill is in, who the members of that committee are, and what district they represent.

Generally, legislative committees work with both grassroots members as well as lobbyists. The combination of the two is very important. First, legislators need to hear both from lobbyists, who are continuously providing information to them, as well as from their constituents at the grassroots level, who will be impacted by the decision. Second, because the lobbyist is at the capitol, attending committees and speaking with legislators, he or she is the eyes and ears of where bills of interest are going at any given time. If an important bill will be coming to a committee the following week, the lobbyist can tell the member organization and the member organization can send out legislative updates to its membership. Without this internal contact, a bill may pass or die without constituents ever having an opportunity to have their voices heard in a timely manner.

Legislative committees are also important because they identify the issues that are likely to come up in future legislative sessions that are of interest to their membership. For TN-NASW, this includes professional bills such as social workers in schools or title protection, as well as bills that affect our clients, such as social program changes. They also look at bills that impact our code of ethics, such as antidiscrimination issues. The legislative committee creates a list of upcoming bills, prioritizes them, and ranks them in order of importance. Top priority is given to any bill that the organization is planning on introducing. The next priority is given to issues that the lobbyist will be advocating for or working against. Then there are issues that we will track. All of these are sent out to the membership so they can act on issues as they arise in committee.

Another important issue that the legislative committee grapples with is resources. Obviously, we cannot actively work on every issue. Therefore the committee will look for other organizations that may be working on the same issue. Do they need help? Should we partner with them? Do they already have a strong coalition? This helps the committee decide whether to actively work on an issue or to track the issue and report back to membership. As previously discussed, the legislative process is a very strategic one, and legislative committees are important in order to bring timely and accurate information back to the member base.

The Social Work Consumer and Title Protection Act outlined previously is a good example of the importance of the legislative committee in strategizing who would oppose or support the bill and deciding whether we would amend the bill to get it to pass. Although we worked to get title protection for all social workers, it was apparent that the legislation would not go through if we attempted to supersede the federal law. Although the bill has passed, the legislative committee will have to continue to track any legislation that may emerge in a new session that tries to amend it further. After the implications became clear for some agencies who had allowed nonsocial workers to assume the title, they began to oppose it. Whether they will eventually try to amend it further will have to be watched carefully by the legislative committee.

Political Action Committees

While 501(c)(3) nonprofit organizations cannot endorse candidates, PACs can. Social workers in nonprofit organizations that cannot endorse candidates for election can often participate in their membership organization's PAC. A PAC is organized specifically to support candidates for election by providing endorsements, financial support, and urging the membership to support the endorsed candidates. While there are many critics of PACs, they can be a useful tool to provide information about candidates and their issues to members, as well as assist candidates who have shown they support our interests in getting elected.

Research indicates that contributions from PACs increase access to legislators, particularly if the organizations' members have ties in their districts, and increase voting behaviors that get candidates into office (Engstrom & Kenney, 2002; Hojnacki & Kimball, 2001). When a PAC endorses a candidate, then, they are supporting candidates they believe in and candidates they believe they can work with after their election. PAC officials have indicated that simply creating obstacles to a politically hostile incumbent's reelection attempts is sometimes the objective of their efforts.

Political Action Committees carefully screen races to determine how their contributions can make the most difference. Endorsements and spending is done strategically, depending on the vulnerability of the incumbent (how safe his or her seat is), and the quality of the challenger. The research also finds that PAC-affiliated groups contact more committee members, and that donations tend to be directed toward legislators serving on committees whose jurisdictions intersect with the PAC's legislative interests. Since member organizations, such as corporations, labor unions, and occupational associations are likely to have ties in multiple districts, and they obviously have legislative interests, they make up a large number of PACs.

The National Association of Social Workers has PACs at both the federal and state legislative levels. As is evidenced by the earlier discussion, endorsing candidates is a very strategic activity. From my experience, NASW endorses candidates who are (a) incumbents who have supported our issues in the past, (b) challengers who may be more sympathetic to our issues than the incumbent, and (c) fence-sitters—someone who has shown promise in supporting our issues in the future. These choices do not always fall along party lines. For example, at the state level, some generally conservative candidates have special areas where they are quite socially progressive. Or, there are legislators who may not vote with us on socially progressive issues, but are allies on professional issues. Thus, the decision to endorse a candidate for election is a complex one, in which the planning process is advantageous. Looking at the potential intended and unintended consequences of supporting one candidate over another as well as the potential obstacles and successes that each candidate may pose to our future legislative agenda must be analyzed for each candidate. Weighing out the pros and cons of each—and for those we decide to endorse, also assessing whether we should endorse with a contribution—are all parts of the decision-making process. PACs are an important vehicle for social workers to utilize. Working within the current legislative process is an important and challenging task; assisting friendly legislators to get into office makes the task easier.

SUMMARY

Although the legislative process is complex, there are many ways that social workers can influence the process. This chapter provides examples of individuals, small groups, and large membership organizations who have influenced the legislative process in significant ways. Using the planning process to outline specific strategies is essential for a number of reasons. It brings complicated tasks down to manageable interventions. It assesses who may be allies working on similar issues, as well as where potential obstacles may lie. It provides a way to evaluate the effort and to change strategy as needed.

Remember that relationships are best built before they are needed. Our representatives live close to us; they are our neighbors, have kids in our schools, and have the same issues at home that we do. They are in office because they want to serve the public interest. It is up to us to assist them by educating them, providing them information, and helping them understand the needs of all persons in our community.

TEST YOURSELF

A. Go to your state legislative web site (if you don't know the web address, Google your "state name" and "legislature" and it will provide you with their web sites. Find out who your senators and representatives are. Read their bios carefully. What committees are they members of? Familiarize yourself with your legislature. Go to the Committees tab and find out what type of committees your legislature has. Go to the Calendars tab. When do committees meet?

B. Suppose there is a bill being proposed in the legislature that would make it illegal for social workers to assist undocumented workers (there was one that was just withdrawn in the federal legislature). You work in a domestic violence shelter. According to this proposed law, you would have to turn away abused women and children if they could not provide papers supporting their legal status. As with so many abused women, they leave with almost nothing, so there would be many women, both undocumented and legal citizens, who might be affected by this legislation. Develop a plan to try to influence the proposed legislation, using the planning process in Chapter 2.

1. Describe the problem.

2. Analyze the problem and the policy change needed.

3. Design a broad goal.

4. Derive measurable objectives to meet the goal.

5. Brainstorm possible strategies and tactics to meet the objectives.

6. Assess the advantages and disadvantages for each possible strategy.

7. Choose the best tactics with the least obstacles.

8. Provide a rationale for your choices.

9. Provide a plan to evaluate your progress toward your goal.

Nine

MONITORING THE BUREAUCRACY AND CREATING CHANGE WITHIN ORGANIZATIONS

Once a bill becomes law, policy practitioners may think that their task is done; it is only the beginning, however, because the law is then sent to the appropriate executive branch agency for interpretation and implementation into a program. Legislative policies are often broad and general in their language; it is then up to the various departments to interpret the broad language and make it specific enough so that programs can be created and implemented. Monitoring this implementation is extremely important and is the next target where intervention can occur. This chapter will examine the implementation process at the executive agency level. The bureaucracy will be examined to identify strategic points of intervention during the regulation-writing phase. The final rules and regulations are then filtered down to local public and private agencies to implement the programs, where agencies often have great latitude in how they interpret the rules.

Haynes and Mickelson (2003) discuss the importance of following the entire process, from passing the law, through the interpretation of the executive agency, and then down to the implementation phase in organizations. They conclude that after legislation is passed, administrative rules may be written "that misinterpret the intent of the law, or [that] agencies may implement the regulations [in a way] that differs from the intent [of the administrative rules]" (p. 139). Therefore, this chapter will deal with interventions at the executive branch level as well as change strategies from within organizations. External organizational change (groups targeting changes in organizations of which they are not employed) was discussed at length in Chapter 7. Here, internal organizational change will be examined, both from a top-down and a bottom-up approach. Top-down approaches are often used to implement new rules and regulations that are required by the executive branch. Effectively dealing with constant changes is challenging for administrators in organizations. Bottom-up approaches are needed when policies and procedures become incongruent with the needs of clients, or when the organization experiences goal displacement, occurring when "agencies over time . . . become preoccupied with their own maintenance and survival" rather than the goals set forth to attain their mission (Galambos, Dulmus, & Wodarski, 2005, p. 63).

Social work administrators are assuming more policy practice roles now than in the past. Haynes and Mickelson (2003) report that decentralization of decision making as well as potential decreases in funding are putting pressure on organizations to compete for survival. Thus, social work administrators are much more involved in both influencing legislative outcomes and administrative rulemaking. Furthermore, because of the changes that decentralization and decreased funding have placed on organizations, they are also more likely to undertake organizational change to more effectively and efficiently provide services.

THE EXECUTIVE BRANCH AND THE BUREAUCRACY

When we think about the executive branch of the government we generally think about the President or Governor. But the executive branch of the government is much larger than the federal or state chief officer. At the federal level the executive branch is made up of 15 executive agencies, of which the head of each sits on the president's cabinet. Rapid Reference 9.1 lists the 15 executive branch agencies that serve under the President.

These agencies make up the bureaucracy of the federal government. Part of their job is to interpret and ensure implementation of the laws passed in the legislative branch. They also serve a regulatory function and carry out executive orders of the president. Because the heads of the

=== *Rapid Reference 9.1*

Federal Executive Agencies

Department of Agriculture	Department of the Interior
Department of Commerce	Department of Justice
Department of Defense	Department of Labor
Department of Education	The State Department
Department of Energy	Department of Transportation
Department of Health and Human Services	Department of the Treasury
Department of Homeland Security	Department of Veterans Affairs
Department of Housing and Urban Development	

executive agencies are appointed by the president, and the bureaucracy itself (the thousands of employees that make up the departments), are not subject to the same pressure of public scrutiny as the legislature, the executive branch agencies appear largely insulated from public pressure. This presents greater challenges for policy practitioners, particularly because it is more difficult to influence the bureaucracy since they are not elected, and their meetings regarding implementation do not have to be public.

The purpose of the rules and regulations process in the executive branch agencies is to translate the intent of the law into specific statements of how the law will be implemented and enforced (McInnis-Dittrich, 1994). Usually the rulemaking process goes to the agency that has the greatest expertise in that particular area. Although most social workers are unfamiliar with interventions at this level, it is important to be involved in the rule-making process. Legislation that is passed that supports a particular client population, for example, can change dramatically in the rule-making process if it is not carefully monitored by its supporters. Professional contact with the staff members assigned to write the administrative rules can critically influence the final regulations.

INTERVENTION AT THE EXECUTIVE LEVEL

As Hoefer (2006) notes, even though there is less research on how to influence the executive branch, the process is somewhat similar to advocating for legislation in terms of working with agencies early in the process, establishing oneself as an expert, gaining a level of trust, and building relationships and networks within the agency. There are two phases during the regulation-writing period that are important. The first is immediately after the law has passed, during the prepublication period. This is the time before the actual comment period, when all stakeholders are invited to comment on the proposed rules in the Federal Register. The second phase is, of course, during the comment period itself. By law, these comments must be considered by regulators and do influence the outcome of the final rules. In Hoefer's (2001) research on interest groups, he found that the most highly effective groups were significantly more likely to offer drafts of regulations to executive agencies prior to publication of the proposed regulations in the Federal Register, as well as taking changes of the proposed regulations to the proposing agency. He suggests that working with agencies before the comment period is an important strategy, because by the time the proposed regulations come out it is difficult to make substantial changes. It is better to follow the legislation immediately into the executive agency and assist them in writing the proposed legislation by offering drafts, statistics, and assistance. If groups wait for the comment period on the proposed regulations, they have much less influence individually than if they work closely with the agency from the beginning.

Another intervention target at the executive agency level is in the implementation of executive orders. Executive orders can change eligibility requirements, administrative procedures, or reduce outreach, effectively bypassing the legislative process. Since the end of World War II, presidents have established administrative agencies and programs through executive orders and reorganization plans that would have never been created through legislative action (Howell & Lewis, 2002). To justify these actions, presidents generally look to some combination of constitutional powers, vague statutes, or expressed delegations of authority. One good example of this is affirmative action. Affirmative action in employment requires changes in hiring and promotion policies. More than 20 years before the Civil Rights Act of 1964 banned employment discrimination based on race, religion, sex, or national origin, President Roosevelt signed an executive order in 1941 requiring defense plants to show they were opening jobs to Black workers. The Kennedy administration coined the term in a ruling that directed firms with federal contracts to take "positive steps" to have a racially representative workforce. By legislating with executive orders, presidents (and governors, for that matter) can require policies that legislators are not ready or willing to pass for political reasons. Executive orders are then turned over to the executive branch agencies to implement programmatically.

Although the same process is used to intervene with the bureaucracy after an executive order, it is different in the sense that there is no legislation to follow, so the organization or interest group must also keep track of policies that may actually originate in the Executive Office.

In 2004, the Office of Management and Budget (OMB) began requiring all executive agency web sites to make information more available and accessible to the public, in accordance with public comment, and to post that information on their web site in order to fulfill the requirements of the E-Government Act of 2002 (P.L. 107-347). This is a useful way for organizations to track and monitor issues to keep up with proposed rules and regulations resulting from both legislation and executive orders.

Executive agency bureaucracies respond to interest group comments for two main reasons. First, interest groups can assist the bureaucracy by providing new information and expertise while drafting rules and implementing programs. Second, when there is some consensus in the information provided to agencies by the public, a clearer message is sent regarding particular rules. In his research on variables that impact the direct influence of interest groups on bureaucratic rules, Yackee (2005) found that the bureaucracy "(1) changes its implementation of public policy to better match the level of government regulation suggested by interest group commenters, (2) incorporates specific policy recommendations of interest groups into its final rules, (3) responds when there is a high level of agreement in the central messages sent within the interest groups, and (4) makes noteworthy changes to rules during the notice and comment period" (p. 118).

PUBLIC STATE AND LOCAL AGENCIES

Oftentimes the regulatory language ultimately used remains intentionally vague if the intent of the law is to give greater autonomy to local and state governments to implement programs in a decentralized manner. Advocates for decentralizing government in this way argue that state and local governments are in a better position than the federal government to assess the needs of the local population. Critics of devolution argue that a strong federal presence is needed to ensure that resources are allocated equitably. As devolution and privatization of services have increased, local agencies have fewer guidelines for implementing programs, resulting in greater variation among agencies in how these programs are delivered.

Programs may be implemented in a public agency, such as public assistance programs through the Department of Human Services, which would be a local branch of the larger Department of Health and Human Services through the executive branch of government. Public agencies at the local level were discussed in detail in Chapter 7 and include agencies such as housing authorities, police departments, planning commissions, and transportation boards. But these agencies receive money and are also regulated by the federal and state government. The local housing authority, for example, is under the umbrella of the local executive branch (e.g., the mayor's office), but is also under Housing and Urban Development (HUD), which interprets laws from the legislature or executive orders from the president, and in turn brings these rules and regulations down to the local housing authorities for implementation.

FOR-PROFIT AND NONPROFIT ORGANIZATIONS

Over the last 30 years, more and more health and social services are implemented through private organizations. These organizations can be not-for-profit or for-profit. The process of shifting dollars away from public governmental agencies to private organizations is called *privatization.* Privatization and devolution are closely related terms, because both shift responsibility away from government, in particular the federal government. The logic behind the movement is that private corporations will be more innovative in their programming and less stagnant than government. The movement toward privatizing services, especially within the for-profit sector of government, is not without controversy, however. For profit, by definition, means that the organization expects to make a profit, generally by reducing costs in order to increase revenues. Regardless of the type of organization, new rules and regulations require internal organizational change in order to remain in compliance with the law.

Internal Organizational Change

Organization's Readiness for Change
Internal organizational change is defined as modifying formal or informal policies, programs, procedures, or management practices. In order for changes to be implemented, each organization must implement new programs or make changes to existing programs. This requires change at all levels of the agency, and change produces stress. Thus, part of the discussion on internal organizational change will center on what researchers have found to be the most efficacious methods for producing healthy change in organizations.

Each organization must be viewed individually and its readiness for change assessed. Barriers to change should be anticipated, and the length of time and commitment needed should not be underestimated. Organizations that use participatory approaches and empowerment strategies will benefit workers and consumers in the long run through a more efficacious workforce that provides strengths and empowerment-based practice to their clients.

Research on an organization's readiness for change suggests that employees must feel that there is a need for change, that they have an opportunity to participate in the change process, and that they have the ability to successfully accomplish the change once it is implemented (Cunningham, Woodward, Shannon et al., 2002). Thus, employees who have limited opportunities for involvement decrease an organization's readiness for change. To increase an organization's readiness for change requires active employee participation, using a problem-solving strategy for planning, and enhancing workers' perceptions of their own ability to cope with the change once it occurs. Carefully review Chapter 3 on interpersonal communication and Chapter 6 on collaboration and trust to make sure that your organization is ready for change. Without taking into consideration issues of interpersonal communication and levels of trust the organization will not be ready for change. Information, communication, cooperation, and sensitivity are valuable tools for ensuring that effective organizational change occurs.

Assessing an organization's readiness for change should be included in the planned change effort. This is an addition needed to the planning process when looking at internal change efforts that may not be in other policy practice projects and should be undertaken during the initial problem identification, where we look for barriers to change in organizations. Before one can begin to implement major changes within an organization it is important to have an understanding of where the organization is culturally, because change from within taps into the relationships among supervisors and staff, upper management and front line workers, and so on. If there is a lack of trust in the organizational culture of the agency, then work must be done to increase trust before the problem-solving model can be used, because the organization is not ready for change.

Another issue that must be addressed when looking at an organization's readiness for change focuses on cultural differences within agencies. As the United States increasingly becomes more multiethnic, organizations must also continue to develop their agencies to address greater multicultural understanding, to value cultural differences, and to transform their goals and activities to reflect a greater depth of respect for those differences. Multicultural organizational development is still in its infancy, but conceptually seeks to reduce patterns of oppression in institutions and organizations. Its focus is on the dynamics of power and oppression at the organizational level, and it requires an assessment of the level of multicultural development that currently exists, from diversity being viewed as a deficit, to being tolerated, to being seen as a strength. The location of an organization on this continuum predicts whether an organization is ready for change, and whether it is capable of establishing more participatory work structures. Hyde (2003) suggests that "efforts that do not challenge and transform core values and processes of an agency allow the status quo to remain. That status quo represents . . . dominant group beliefs, perspectives and actions" (p. 43). Agencies that make only superficial change are ultimately mistrusted by clients and the community. Developing multicultural competence in organizations is a long-term process that requires a continuous monitoring process to evaluate an organization's readiness for higher-level intergroup relationships.

Resistance to change by both employees and employers occurs for several reasons:

- People resist changing old habits.
- Initiating change requires large investments of time.
- Change may be interpreted as questioning competence.
- Change threatens values and beliefs.

Internal Organizational Change from the Top Down

Once the organization's readiness for change is assessed, organizational planned change efforts can occur. Most organizational change occurs from the top down. Human service agencies must respond to variations in the political and social environment that put internal and external pressure on organizations to modify their formal policies and programs (Galambos, Dulmus, & Wodarski, 2005). These can come in the forms of changes in laws, rules and regulations (as discussed previously), changes in funding streams, or changes in the characteristics of those using services.

D'Aprix and Gay (2006) list several common responses by employees to organizational change:

- Early adapters: These are among the first people to get on board and embrace change. They are often important leaders who may be able to influence others to accept or embrace the change.
- The early majority: These people recognize the necessity for change and tend to be optimistic that change may make things better.
- Fence sitters: These are the undecided employees who are not against change, but want to wait and see how it will play out.
- The late majority: Must be convinced that the change is positive, and are worried about how it will affect them personally. The late majority will go along with change once they are convinced that it will be positive.
- The late adapters: Some of these will never accept the change and will remain in denial. If they are not eventually brought into the fold, they become a toxic part of the employee population and will remain in opposition.

It is obvious from looking at the different ways people will handle change that organizational change not only includes changing policies and procedures, but changing people's attitudes and behaviors. The success of any change effort depends on how much people can change their attitudes to be consistent with the changing needs and goals of the organization. In order for this to occur, there are several issues that must be addressed for employees to buy into organizational change.

In Stollar, Poth, Curtis, and Cohen's (2006) review of the literature on recent legislative changes in education, they found several reasons why schools were unsuccessful at implementing changes required by new rules and regulations. Rapid Reference 9.2 delineates why changes, although required by law, may still fail.

Communication is the first key to success. Employees need information as to why there is a need for change (rules and regulations have changed, granting requirements have changed, etc.), and management needs information on how employees experience the front lines, so that change actually meets the needs of the organization and its clients. Several of the failures noted earlier could be avoided with appropriate communication.

Collaboration requires a team-based approach to planning for change. Collaboration enhances the probability that people will understand the need for change, and that they will feel they have been able to participate in the planning and implementation of the new procedures. Employee participation "increases employee support for the change, prevents burnout, and addresses underlying factors of trust, dependence and resistance to change" (Galambos, Dulmus, & Wodarski, 2005, p. 75).

Adequate time must be allotted for the process of planning internal organizational change. Inadequate time allowed to plan and implement changes may pose major problems for the organization. Rushing into

≡ *Rapid Reference 9.2*

Why Mandated Changes Fail

- Initiative is not followed by continuous communication.
- If there is inadequate time for implementation.
- If the change is not well matched to the culture of the organization.
- If personnel do not see the need for change, do not understand the problem that the change is supposed to address.
- If people who must implement the change lack an understanding of the new procedures.
- If training is not provided.

any major organizational change without time to think through potential unintended consequences is a mistake. Because collaboration and communication both require time up front, effective internal change will be compromised if there is not time for reflective thinking, processing, and participation.

Empowerment Practice as a Change Strategy in Agencies

Leadership style and organizational structure both impact the efficacy of staff in helping clients. Staff members who feel empowered within the agency are more likely to effectively empower their clients by recognizing oppression and working together to combat social injustice. There is a link of empowerment and the strengths perspective, in which a practitioner focuses on what resources a person has and then teaches them to use those resources (Dewees, 1999). If staff feel disempowered they will be less likely to provide the most effective interventions and services to their clients (Bednar, 2003). What employees receive both personally and professionally from their organization will in turn determine the level of empowerment they feel in their jobs. In order to effectively develop programs that work, empowerment of employees is a necessary step.

The top-down, bureaucratic nature of most organizations creates an environment where employees have a greater tendency to become powerless. As with powerlessness seen in clients, the problems of vulnerability, loss of control, and a sense of helplessness create an environment of powerlessness for workers (Shera & Page, 1995). This type of environment will pose greater challenges for administrators who need to implement effective organizational change.

The benefits of implementing empowerment strategies in an organizational context are becoming increasingly evident. Empowerment has received attention in all areas—business, management, and the human services. "An empowered agency structure is one in which leadership and responsibilities are shared, communication and interaction patterns are based on principles of empowerment, and organizational changes are possible from below as well as from the upper levels of the organization" (Shera & Page, 1995, p. 3). Empowerment practice should be integrated into all levels of an organization's activities.

The implementation of empowerment practice at the organizational level requires the use of participatory management techniques as well as an organizational culture that is based on partnership and mutual respect. Important to the definition of organizational empowerment is the facilitation of a process that leads to "realized (not simply perceived) control" (Foster-Fisherman & Keys, 1997, p. 347). O'Connor (2002) suggests that too often, definitions of empowerment in the literature direct attention away from concrete participation, control and rights, to psychological conditions, such as feelings, beliefs, or a state of mind. Therefore, organizational empowerment is largely defined by the extent that management is willing and able to grant authority, decision making, autonomy, access to information, creativity, and responsibility to their employees (Petter, Byrnes, & Choi, 2002).

Guterman and Bargal (1996) suggest the following organizational principles are needed to implement empowerment practice in an organization: (1) staff development opportunities, like advanced training and support for actualizing the special interests and talents of workers, (2) a collaborative, teamlike approach among colleagues, (3) a safe organizational environment that allows workers to openly address difficult concerns, (4) a shared organizational philosophy and commitment of the agency, (5) supervisory leadership that communicates support for and positive feedback regarding workers' efforts, and (6) administrative recognition and validation of workers' efforts through promotions, good salaries, and comfortable physical working conditions. The increase in power has to occur at all levels within the organization for clients and staff to be truly empowered.

Likewise, Gutierrez, GlenMaye, and DeLois (1995) found that staff development, enhanced collaborative approach, and administrative leadership and support are tactics that can help change traditional attitudes and make way for new ways of thinking among staff. Rapid Reference 9.3

≡ *Rapid Reference 9.3*

Essential Components of Empowerment in Organizations

- Collaborative team approach to decision making
- Education and advanced training opportunities
- Flexible hours and good compensation
- An environment of support and recognition from colleagues
- Fostering a community-based approach in service delivery
- Creating smaller units or teams that have decision-making authority

delineates the essential components of empowerment in organizations. Advanced training and in-service training, such as access to conferences, training, and educational opportunities, being given encouragement and opportunities to develop programs and professional skills that match personal interests, being rewarded through promotions and salary increases for pursuing self-defined learning goals, and the provision of flexible hours and encouragement toward self-care are all options that can educate staff and develop empowerment capacity. The use of peer supervision and review to build relationships and support systems among staff strengthens the horizontal structure of the organization.

The implementation of empowerment practice does not occur overnight, because it involves a paradigm shift at all levels within an organization. Empowerment practice, however, is worth the time investment because the investment is people. Researchers have shown the correlation between worker empowerment and client outcomes. Organizations have a responsibility to provide the best possible service to clients; therefore, implementing empowerment practice is necessary to best meet the needs of clients as well as staff.

A full commitment of the organization, both administration and staff, is necessary in moving toward empowerment practice. Administrators play a key role in setting the pace and sustaining an environment that utilizes empowerment approaches, but staff may not initially embrace empowerment models, so effective training and collaboration techniques are required at all levels of the organization for empowerment-based changes to occur.

DON'T FORGET

You cannot lead if you do not know the will of your workers. You cannot know the will of your workers if they are not permitted to express that will by questioning your leadership. Intimidation is not leadership. Establish a trusting culture and workers will create solutions to problems by pursuing their own competence.

Fisher (1999).

Internal Organizational Change from the Bottom Up

Very little has been written on internal organizational change from the bottom up. Employees often want to change policies, programs, or procedures, but most agencies do not have a structure in place to assist with a bottom-up approach to organizational change. Bottom-up change from within is full of uncertainty. Workers may risk being fired or ostracized by colleagues if they are not particularly thoughtful during the planning stages. Changing organizations from the ground up uses all of the strategies discussed earlier, but also must be done very strategically. The problem-solving model from Chapter 2 is appropriate for use in bottom-up change, but must be done with great care and sensitivity. Schneider and Lester (2001) provide additional tips for workers who wish to pursue organizational change.

- Communication—Interpersonal skills are essential (see Chapter 3). Have the ability to assess your coworkers and upper-level administrators accurately. Avoid careless language. Choose your words carefully. Anticipate how you will impact others.
- Get the facts—Use research, best practices, and results of internal evaluations to help make your case.

- Plan strategies and tactics—Promote innovations in agencies by initiating new ideas through program development. Be prepared to show how the change can be financed. Come prepared with cost-benefit analyses.
- Broaden base of support—Focus on collaboration within the agency. As with the change strategies from the top, use participatory practices to include ideas of others who would also like to see change occur.
- Be persistent—Achieve change over time. Just as with legislative change, or other organizational change, it is often slow and incremental. Do not lose hope; doing nothing is surely slower!
- As with all planned change efforts, continually evaluate your progress and adjust your plans as necessary.

The following Putting It Into Practice illustrates an organizational change strategy undertaken by university students to try to make their building handicapped accessible. Targeting the university is a huge goal. Although they desired fundamental change, the students were able to make incremental changes immediately, but their larger goal would take another 7 years to attain.

The task force faced resistance from the university in several departments while they were trying to get information for their project. Working for change from within creates a tension between people who would normally want to help, but are put in a conundrum because of the political nature of the change. Employees may be fearful if they give out information that could be used to create conflict. It was interesting that the task force chose very nonconfrontational tactics in educating the university community, and then the pressure actually came from the very groups that became educated.

The changes those students saw back in the mid-1990s were very incremental. The sidewalk curbs were fixed, more handicapped parking spaces were secured, and a promise of a more timely renovation plan was given. If any of those students recognize this story, I will tell you to stop by the

Putting It Into Practice

Change from Below: The Case of Handicapped Accessibility

Planned Change Model for Organizational Change

Problem Identification: The student Handicapped Accessibility Task Force at the University wanted to make changes so that their building would be handicapped accessible under the Americans with Disabilities Act (ADA), Title II, requiring all public universities to make services, programs, and activities accessible. The Reasonable Accommodation clause in the ADA appeared to be a loophole, allowing universities to remain incompliant without having to make many changes. For example, rather than making a building accessible, classes were moved to other buildings that were accessible.

Identify needed advocacy effort: The students wanted to create a greater sense of urgency within the university to begin making more accommodations for students. The university had a 20-year plan in place for making accommodations. The social work building's remodeling was originally scheduled for the 18th year.

Determining the target for change, assessing the organization's readiness for change: Because this was an internal organizational change, the Handicapped Accessibility Task Force targeted the university for change, but also chose incremental change strategies, because the university had fiscal problems and the task force felt that the university was not ready for more fundamental change.

The broad goal of the advocacy effort: The broad goal of their project was to create a more accessible campus in general, and to create greater accessibility in the social work building in particular.

Objectives chosen: The original objectives were incremental: (a) to create awareness among the administration of the challenges of physically disabled students and possible program developments that could occur to make the social work building more handicapped accessible, and (b) to educate and garner support of the student body for greater disability access. As you will see shortly, the project began to take on a life of its own.

(continued)

Possible intervention strategies/tactics/activities: The students brainstormed several approaches to attain their objectives, such as demonstrations and distributing grievance forms to disabled students, but decided that these were too adversarial when less confrontational methods were still available to them. They ultimately decided to use the media, fliers, and brochures to get the message out to the university community, and to write a proposal for a more timely accessibility plan to provide the student government with. They also developed several alternative methods to create greater accessibility in their own building, including an elevator and a chair lift proposal. In organizational change, having more than one alternative for administrators to choose from is important. They had engineers come in to determine what each idea would entail and detailed costs and benefits of each.

Implementation: As they educated students on campus, more organizations became interested in the effort. Their articles were published in the university newspaper and on the Chancellor's Discussion Page on the Internet. The Social Work Student Organization decided to continue to take up the issue after the task force disbanded at the end of the semester. Handicapped students began contacting the task force, wanting to become involved.

Outcomes: The outcomes of the effort were interesting. The local news media picked up the issue and decided to interview one of the students in the social work building who was in a wheelchair. It made the front page, along with a picture of the student in his wheelchair at the bottom of the steps. The Social Work Organization held a forum on handicapped accessibility which also brought news attention, as 20 or so wheelchair-bound students crammed into a small conference room. The university decided to create more handicapped parking spaces closer to the building, created wheelchair-accessible curbs at the street, and changed the social work building's accessibility renovation status from being on the 18-year plan to a 5-year plan.

social work building now. Seven years after this task force completed their project, we went through a year-long renovation of our building. All the classrooms, the offices, and the student lounge are now accessible. And we have a GREAT elevator. Change takes time. Sometimes social workers cannot see their change efforts surface right away and become frustrated, but I always tell students, when working at the macro level, change can come, but it is very slow.

Whether the organizational change is occurring from the top down or the bottom up, it is apparent that the organization's readiness for change must be assessed during the planning process. Internal organizational change presents different challenges than externally focused change on organizations. The dynamics are very different when one is attempting to change a system that she or he works in on a daily basis.

SUMMARY

From the legislature down to the local agency, there is a continuum that occurs to put a policy into action. At each stage, social workers must keep working for programs to be developed and implemented in a way that the law intended. While the executive branch's rules and regulations comment period offers a window of opportunity to influence change, these rules still must be developed into programs. Internal organizational change is a challenge to develop new programs to fulfill agency mandates. The process by which that development takes place often predicts the success or failure of the outcome. Effective internal organizational change takes a participatory structure and attempts to use empowerment methods to get staff on board for the best program outcomes to occur.

🖋 TEST YOURSELF 🖋

A. Go to the Federal Register (it is available online, just Google "federal register"). On the Federal Register home page, click on Rules and Regulations. In the search put in volume 66 page 28776 through 28779. These are the proposed rules for the Zero Tolerance "One Strike and You're Out" policy under the Anti Drug Abuse Act of 1998. You can see the comments that organizations sent in to respond to the proposed rules created by HUD, and how HUD decided to deal with them.

(continued)

B. Break up into two groups. One group is administrative staff, the other frontline staff. Decide on a problem in the organization that needs to be changed. Use the planning process from Chapter 2 to outline a strategy for change.

   1. Describe the problem.

   2. Analyze the problem and the policy change needed.

   3. Design a broad goal.

   4. Derive measurable objectives to meet the goal.

   5. Brainstorm possible strategies and tactics to meet the objectives.

   6. Assess the advantages and disadvantages for each possible strategy.

   7. Choose the best tactics with the least obstacles.

   8. Provide a rationale for your choices.

   9. Provide a plan to evaluate your progress toward your goal.

 10. How different are the change strategies, depending on whether you belong to the administrative group or the employee group?

Ten

ESSENTIALS OF JUDICIAL POLICY PRACTICE

The judiciary is the third branch of the government, consisting of court systems at the local, state, and federal levels. The judicial system is inherently political. Judges are either appointed or elected. If they are elected, their principles reflect the values of the voters; if they are appointed, they reflect the political ideology, to some degree, of the elected official who appoints them. One need only look at the historic battles over U.S. Supreme Court nominations to see how political the selection of federal judges is. Most people do not think of the courts as policymakers, but indeed they are. Policymaking in the court rests with the judges' power to interpret the law. If a law is passed in the legislature, for example, the courts can overturn it if they find it to be unconstitutional or illegal, based on other laws. Judges' personal and political values cannot be divorced from this process. Although judges are bound to follow the rulings of higher courts in earlier cases in their jurisdiction, many cases arise where there is a gap, conflict, or ambiguity in the language of the law or of earlier cases interpreting it. In those cases, courts cannot avoid having their politics and values play a role in their choices about the proper interpretation of the law. These opinions, if not overturned in a higher court, then function as precedent for later cases.

This chapter will first introduce the reader to the court system, how the three branches of government interact to create policy, and how they function to monitor and balance one another. Change strategies at the judicial branch can take two forms. The courts can be a targeted system for change or they can be utilized as an avenue to change another branch of the government or a private organization. Both of these potential avenues for change will be explored and the skills needed for successful interventions described.

THE COURT SYSTEM

The Federal System

The Supreme Court is the highest court in the federal system because it is the final step available for appeal. The Supreme Court hears most cases on appeal from a lower court. Rapid Reference 10.1 gives the breakdown of the federal system. The next lower level of the federal court system is the 13 U.S. Courts of Appeals, also known as circuit courts. They take appeals from federal trial courts, the lowest level in the federal system, known as the Federal District Courts. Therefore, if a person is involved in a suit in U.S. court, the case will be heard by a district court first. If one of the parties is dissatisfied and can point to an error of law that the party believes occurred at the trial court level, the case can be appealed to a Federal Court of Appeals (Appellate Court) in their circuit (Maerowitz & Mauet, 2003). If the plaintiff (or the defendant) is still dissatisfied, they may appeal to the Supreme Court for review, although the Supreme Court reviews only a small number of cases, and only if they involve matters of national concern or conflicting outcomes in different appellate courts.

Judges at the federal level are

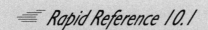

Rapid Reference 10.1

Breakdown of the Federal Court System

U.S. Supreme Court

Hears appeals from appellate courts or original cases of important national interest.

↑

U.S. Courts of Appeals

Hears cases appealed from federal district courts.

↑

Federal District Trial Courts

Hears cases regarding constitutional questions, federal laws, or interstate cases.

appointed for life, with the advice and consent of the Senate. Usually a panel of three judges will hear cases in the U.S. Courts of Appeal. In the U.S. Supreme Court there is one chief justice and eight associate justices who hear cases. The U.S. Supreme Court primarily hears appeals from lower courts, and hears some original cases, if they have to do with treason or disputes between states. The U.S. Supreme court has the right to hear or refuse cases brought to it on appeal. The court is more likely to accept a case if the subject presents a basic constitutional issue or if different appellate courts have heard similar cases but ruled inconsistently on constitutional issues. In general, the U.S. Supreme Court takes only cases that have sufficient national significance to warrant its attention or to resolve conflict between appellate courts.

The State Court System

The state court system has a similar structure and composition as the federal court system. Beginning with the lower, or inferior, courts, there are municipal courts and county (or parish) courts, which generally conduct trials in minor civil or criminal cases. Courts of general jurisdiction make up the second tier of the state court systems. These are trial courts that hear civil and criminal cases as well as conducting new trials brought to them from inferior courts. The third tier of courts at the state level is the appellate court system (Courts of Appeals), which hear appeals from the district courts. Finally, as with the federal system, the highest state court is the State Supreme Court. In some cases, an appeal from a state supreme court to the U.S. Supreme Court may be possible if there are federal issues involved.

Although all states differ somewhat, most of the judges at the local level are elected. Appellate and supreme courts justices are elected or appointed. If judges are appointed then they have retention elections after a certain number of years, depending on the state. In Tennessee, for example, appellate court judges sit in panels of three and are appointed by the Governor, based on nominations from a Judicial Selection Commission. There are five supreme court justices and four associate justices, appointed by the Governor for an 8-year term. All appointed judges then have retention votes.

Interconnectedness of the Three Branches of Government

The three branches of government have checks on one another, and no decision by any one branch is absolute. For example, the U.S. Congress can amend the Constitution in a way that might overturn specific Supreme Court decisions. At the state level, constitutions can also be amended that may overturn a supreme court decision. Legislatures can also pass laws to systemize the court system, such as mandatory sentencing laws for certain drug-related crimes. The executive branch (at the federal level) can appoint federal judges who share their beliefs and philosophy if an appointment is available during the president's term, but the Senate must confirm the nomination.

The main check that the courts have over legislatures is that they have the power to rule that a law passed by the legislature is unconstitutional or is in conflict with another law. One well-known exercise of this judicial power is *Brown v. the Board of Education,* a case that challenged racial segregation in public school. Racial segregation had been upheld by the U.S. District Court because of the precedent set by earlier rulings based on segregation laws in Louisiana. But upon appeal, the U.S. Supreme Court found that the separate but equal doctrine that had been upheld earlier violated the fourteenth amendment of the U.S. Constitution, thus opening the door to school integration. This is an example of how no state constitution may violate the federal Constitution and also of the use of the courts to interpret the constitutionality of legislative law, both state and federal.

The courts also have checks on the executive branch as well, particularly the writing of administrative rules and regulations by executive agencies, discussed in Chapter 9. The rules of the executive branch agencies are subject to judicial review to ensure they accurately carry out the original intent of the law as passed in the legislature. The courts also have authority, once the rules are written, to review whether administrative agencies implement them according to the law. This comes through individual or class litigation and will be subsequently discussed. For now, it is important to note that each branch of the government has both checks on it from other branches and has the ability to influence other branches as well. This structure provides a variety of ways for policy practitioners to influence government systems. If one system is not responsive to change, other systems can be used to influence change in a different way. Here are some examples of creating change through the court system, either by advocating change within the courts, or by using the courts as a vehicle for change in other systems.

Change Strategies in the Judicial Branch

The first intervention strategy discussed is targeting the courts for change. Then I will discuss ways to use the judicial branch as a vehicle for change within other systems. Targeting the judicial branch of government can take a number of forms. If one wants to deter certain persons from getting a position in the court, the first step is to assess whether that particular position is elected or appointed.

When judges are appointed, the target system would be the legislature and the executive (either the president or governor, depending on the judge). The strategies outlined in Chapter 8 are key to influencing legislative appointments. For example, in the case of the federal judiciary, contacting leaders through phone calls and letters, using the media to arouse public interest, and using technology to spread the word about potential nominees is important for lobbying both the executive and the Senate Judiciary Committee, since appointments must have the consent of the Senate at the federal level. At the state and local level, because most judges are elected, the first change strategy is to vote. A next step, using the strategies from Chapter 7, is to organize others and provide information on the record of the judicial candidate so that others vote as well. At the state level, even supreme court justices must at some time have a retention vote.

The judicial election has become very political and makes judges vulnerable to lobbying efforts. There is rising concern that elections for judgeships have become too political. The American Bar Association (ABA, 2003) warns that special-interest groups have increased their attempts to influence judicial elections through financial contributions and attack campaigning. It further argues that public trust in the courts is eroding, and the public is increasingly skeptical that judges are neutral arbiters, seeing them instead as political decision makers who too often go beyond their intended role of simply interpreting and applying the existing law. Even those who understand that some degree of political interpretation and value judgment is inherent in judging are worried that the current climate in judicial elections is undermining judicial independence in a way that threatens the checks and balances that are intended to stabilize and guard our democracy.

On one hand, the ABA urges states to take steps to reduce the influence that money and partisan politics have had in judicial election. On the other hand, because 80 percent of judges must stand for election at some point and the majority of the public supports judicial elections, policy practitioners must do what they can to make sure that there is an informed electorate and that reliable information about judges' records reach the voters. As long as judges continue to be elected and there is evidence that they are influenced by interest groups, social workers must continue to attempt to educate the public and influence voting patterns, just as with any other elected official.

TARGETING THE COURTS FOR CHANGE

Once a judge sits on the bench, there are still ways to target the court system for change. Following are two important strategies for change at the judicial level: monitoring the courts and implementing new court programs and procedures.

Monitoring the Court System

Coalitions and citizen groups have worked together to monitor courts when they feel that a judge may not be ruling in the best interest of clients or in the best interests of victims. Mothers Against Drunk Driving (MADD) may be the most well-known example of court monitoring. Their monitoring program trains volunteers to observe and gather information on DUI/DWI court proceedings. The goal of the program is to compile information on how DUI/DWI cases are handled across the country and convey to the legal system that the public is watching how the cases are handled. According to Downes (2004), monitoring works. She reports on research in Maine that indicates when a MADD court monitor is present, the conviction rates for offenders increases by 10 percent and dismissals decrease by 70 percent. Their monitoring program is very comprehensive and focuses on three areas: (1) evaluating the courts on their treatment of victims, understanding of the law, and the manner in which the proceedings were held, (2) tracking information on offender's charges, previous charges and convictions, punishment rendered in any previous convictions, and the offender's demeanor during the proceeding, and (3) information such as plea bargains, the victim's role in the plea agreement, punishment rendered, and whether a victim impact statement was allowed to be read in the courtroom.

The National Council for Adoption (2005) also monitors court performance in foster care placement cases. Their purpose is different from MADD in that they want to create performance measures to provide strategic information to (1) enable the courts to evaluate themselves and develop effective strategies for improvement and (2) enable policymakers, child welfare advocates, and the public to promote successful models for court improvement.

Some caution should be used here. As with any attempt to implement a change strategy, it is important to look at both the goals of monitoring and to investigate in depth the pros and cons of the strategies used. The last thing a group wants to do is to alienate the court, the district attorney, or the defense attorneys involved in the cases. It is important to convey the message that, although your group is monitoring the court, it is understood that all parties involved are doing the best that they can. Do not question their intelligence or their integrity. Furthermore, it is important to analyze specifically what outcome the group wants to attain. In the case of DUI, for example, is the best outcome to lose one's driving privileges for a year? Or would it be best to mandate that they are on intensive probation, and may only drive to work and Alcoholics Anonymous (AA) meetings each week? Interest groups who decide to monitor the court have the victims in mind, but as social workers we must remember that the rights of the accused must also be preserved. Careful analysis of these issues and all potential strategies must be examined in order to find the most desired long-term outcome for all those involved.

The following Putting It Into Practice provides an in-depth examination of the planning process for a monitoring program in a rural court system that a Domestic Violence Task Force decided to implement. The judge was not interested in providing information about resources to domestic violence victims, and some advocates went so far as to say the victims were revictimized when they went to court. Victims did not understand how to procure orders of protection and there was no one in the court to explain the system to them.

The task force was careful to place the focus of the monitoring program on education and information for victims, rather than on the judge's behavior. They were smart to do a thorough assessment of the problem and analyze potential negative consequences of creating a hostile environment within the court. Inviting interested court system stakeholders, such as the district attorney's office, into the process was a good idea politically. It may only be a matter of time until the judge sees the benefits of the program and chooses to participate and take ownership of the project in his own way. In the meantime, the monitors in the courtroom help to control the judge's negative behavior toward victims because he is known to be on his best behavior when there are visitors in the courtroom.

Implementing New Programs within the Court

Coalitions and citizen groups can work with court systems to create new programs within the judicial system. Drug courts, for example, were

Putting It Into Practice

Monitoring the Courts

The target system for the task force was a rural county court that dealt with domestic violence. The problem was that, aside from unprofessional conduct by the judge, the system was not victim friendly—there was no system set up to provide information on orders of protection or other important information that victims of domestic violence need during this process.

- The broad goal of the task force was to implement a court watch program.

- The objectives were to increase fair and dignified treatment of victims and court workers, to train and educate community court watch volunteers, and to implement a weekly precourt educational session for victims. This entails what to expect during a request for an order of protection and a short summary of how things are handled in a courtroom.

- Several intervention strategies were discussed to meet the objectives, always keeping in mind the political atmosphere of the court. For example, utilizing media attention would have been an easier way to find volunteers, but the task force did not want to inflame already difficult circumstances in the courtroom. The strategies chosen to fulfill the objectives were as follows:

  1. Organize known supporters into a coalition to plan the court watch program. This included the district attorney's office, the local Domestic Violence Task Force, and the local domestic violence shelter.

  2. Complete guidelines of roles and responsibilities for court watch volunteers, including guidelines of conduct in the courtroom and what activities they should accomplish.

  3. Provide a complete curriculum for the precourt presentation for victims, including dialogue to use and overhead slides outlining what victims can expect.

Because the district attorney was part of the coalition there was a natural conduit to the judge. Even though there was no interest at this point by the judge, the hope was that by keeping him in the loop of activities that he might take an interest at some point. The district attorney's office also changed the required time to arrive for court to provide time for the presentation before court began. The coalition also began the search for volunteers within their network of interested stakeholders.

formed through diverse coalitions of law enforcement, judges, district attorneys, substance abuse agencies, and citizen groups. These specialized courts seek to prevent incarceration and facilitate treatment for offenders. According to Tyuse and Linhorst (2005), since 1989, 1,238 drug courts are in operation or in the planning stages in all 50 states. As with most pilot programs, after exhibiting effectiveness, the coalitions lobbied Congress, and the development of new drug courts began to be funded in 1994, 5 years after the first drug court was established. There are a multitude of programs that have been implemented in local jurisdictions through coalitions and citizen-group advocacy targeting the court system, including mental health courts, collaborative divorce programs, mediation centers, and other diversion programs.

Some critics of specialized courts suggest that specialized criminal courts encourage special interest control of the court system and, although theoretically designed for rehabilitation, make the court system more punitive. Furthermore, critics suggest that specialized courts often have prescribed sentences without looking at the individual circumstances of each case. Finally, many of the social services available in sentencing are only available after one is arrested, such that many individuals "would likely take advantage of these services on their own if they were packaged as comprehensively as they are in [the] community courts" (Quinn, 2006, p. 665).

In an interview with two local attorneys who have spent a great deal of time trying to implement new innovative programs in local court systems, they caution the reader to look closely at potential unintended consequences of programs that are developed (Wiersema & LeVasseur, personal communication, 10/18/06). It is important to use the planning model to assess the problem, look at many alternatives, and try to foresee unanticipated outcomes that might occur in any new program development effort. Wiersema and LeVasseur also offer skills for working successfully within the court system, which are outlined in Rapid Reference 10.2. These skills should by now sound fairly familiar to the reader, discussed in Chapter 3 on the importance of interpersonal skills in policy practice.

≡ Rapid Reference 10.2

Skills for Working with the Court System

- Rational arguments: Innovative programs do not take power away from the court, but instead decrease the number on the docket.
- Relationship building: It is important to include a diverse range of stakeholders in a task group or coalition of a community problem for which a new program might be needed, particularly the district attorney, judges, and resource groups from the community.
- Interpersonal skills: See members of the target system as doing the best they can. Be willing to listen to their rationale, and don't question their integrity.
- Be creative: Use the planning strategy to brainstorm ideas that might help solve the problem.
- Be persistent: Change takes time. As one of the attorneys stated, "Ask for it so many times it starts to sound normal."

USING THE COURT SYSTEM AS A VEHICLE FOR CHANGE IN OTHER TARGET SYSTEMS

As discussed earlier, if a law is passed in the legislature, the courts can overturn the law if it is found to be unconstitutional or illegal on the basis of other laws. If the rules and regulations promulgated by the executive branch are not found to be in line with the original intent of the law, the rules can be challenged in court as well. If there is a dispute about the proper interpretation of a given law, this dispute can also be brought to a court for resolution. These challenges are brought by the initiation of a lawsuit, sometimes by individual plaintiffs and sometimes through a class action lawsuit brought on behalf of a group of people similarly situated. Discussed in the following are, first, how interest groups have used the courts to monitor the actions of government or private entities, and then a more in-depth look at the different strategies through which monitoring occurs.

Using the Courts to Monitor the Other Branches of Government

The rules and regulations written by executive agencies are subject to judicial review to ensure that the programs conceived by the rules and regulations actually follow the legislature's intent in passing the law. Yackee (2005) found that formal participation of interest groups during the comment period of the rule making process may alter the content of policy because of the threat of future court action. Because judges evaluate whether a final rule was a logical outgrowth of the comments of the proposed rules, by registering their views on the record interest groups provide documentation for later appeals of the regulation. As a result, agencies sometimes take interest group comments very seriously.

After the rules and regulations have been given and agencies are implementing the programs, how the policy is being implemented is also subject to judicial review. However, Canes-Wrone (2003) found that bureaucratic decisions about policy implementation are predicated, to a large degree, on whether the courts will uphold those decisions. Of course, it is not always easy for anyone, bureaucrats included, to predict what courts will do in the future. On the one hand, agencies are certainly aware that administrative law generally requires courts to give them broad discretion and to refrain from intervening in their work unless abuse of discretion has occurred. On the other hand, on occasion an agency is given so much discretion that a court may find the statute or rule in question is unlawful because it is overly vague, providing no standards that members of the community can use to guide their conduct. This is interesting because, as noted in Chapter 9, the legislature has given much broader discretion to agency decision making in a time of devolution of responsibility to the local level.

Interest groups should certainly be aware, in any event, that litigation is one tool that may be available for challenging administrative practices, but the range of situations in which such litigation will succeed is limited. Some groups may choose litigation even when the chance of success is not great because the litigation can provide a public forum that draws attention and dramatizes the issue. Policy-oriented litigation is likely to have much greater impact if it is undertaken as part of a broader strategy that includes community action and strategic use of media to reach the public.

The "One Strike and You're Out" policy under the Anti-Drug Abuse Act of 1998 (42 U.S.C. 1437d(I)(6)), as interpreted in the Rules and Regulations promulgated by the Department of Housing and Urban Development (HUD), was purposely kept vague in order to give housing authorities maximum control over administering the one strike policy. Numerous court challenges have followed since the final rules were published in the Federal register. The following Putting It Into Practice provides an example of how interest

Putting It Into Practice

The Case of Rucker versus Davis

In 1998 Pearl Rucker, a sixty-three-year-old woman who had lived in public housing with her mentally disabled daughter, two grandchildren, and one great-granddaughter was given an eviction notice by the Oakland Housing Authority (OHA) because her daughter was found in possession of cocaine three blocks from the public housing apartment. According to the Anti-Drug Abuse Act as amended in 1998, "any drug related criminal activity on or off such premises, engaged in by a public housing tenant, any member of the tenant's household or any guest or other person under the tenant's control, shall be cause for termination of tenancy."

When HUD issued the regulations for that section they made it clear that public housing authorities (PHAs) should have discretion to consider the circumstances of the case. In response to OHA's actions, Rucker filed in federal district court under the Administrative Practices Act, stating that the statute does not authorize the eviction of innocent tenants, and if it does authorize such evictions, then the statute is unconstitutional. The district court found in favor of the tenants, and OHA appealed the decision to the United States Court of Appeals, who also found in their favor, stating that HUD's interpretation of the law was contrary to congressional intent. In their ruling, the court went on to say "Although the statute permits 'termination of tenancy' it does not answer the question of whose tenancy. While the policy considerations pointed out by the dissent may apply to the eviction of culpable tenants, we do not believe they support the eviction of innocent ones."

groups have challenged the final rules of HUD as they pertain to evictions due to criminal activity of household members and guests of public housing tenants, and how that has affected bureaucratic decision making.

During the comment phase of the rules and regulations pertaining to the law, HUD chose to leave the language regarding "members of tenants' households, or any guest or other person under the tenant's control" purposefully vague because they believed the intent of the law was to give housing authorities latitude in making decisions on an individual basis. This decision ultimately left the language vague enough that it has been challenged repeatedly in court. Although the plaintiffs won the case in the Federal appellate court, it was ultimately overturned by the U.S. Supreme Court. Nevertheless, the number of lawsuits filed in connection with this HUD rule has been such that local housing authorities are re-evaluating their policies regarding this and other language in the rules in order to avoid further lawsuits (Johns, 2002; Wilson, 2005).

Individual Litigation

As evidenced earlier, reform can come through litigation. For instance, parties may succeed in getting a court to strike down a statute or local ordinance or government practice as unconstitutional. They may succeed in showing that an administrative regulation or agency action is an abuse of discretion. They may prove that some public or private entity has violated a law, such as the Americans with Disabilities Act. Courts sometimes have the power to protect citizens against excesses by policing encroachment on individual rights. Litigation is a slow process, however, and it is constrained by legal precedent and by the preference of the court. Social workers desiring to practice policy in this area need to work closely with experts in law, for example the American Civil Liberties Union, legal defense funds, and legal services. The typical role of the social work policy practitioner in litigation, whether it is individual litigation or class actions, is to assist in establishing the case, collecting and interpreting the evidence, organizing public support, establishing accountability, and evaluating outcomes (McInnis-Dittrich, 1994).

Litigation is often used to test cases before the court. With greater privatization of services and more for-profit corporations taking over the responsibility of providing social services, litigation is increasingly being used to challenge unresponsive service systems. Managed health care is an example of using the judicial system to reform the health care system (Lens, 2002). Complaints that profit-driven health care has resulted in reduced access to physicians and denial of necessary medical services to patients have prompted lawsuits against nearly every major managed care company. The nursing home industry has also seen a stark increase in the number of individual lawsuits filed against them (Studdert & Stevenson, 2004). Unlike medical malpractice suits, nursing home litigation centers around abuse and neglect. Given that the medical care received by most residents is quite low, the litigation around nursing homes concerns the lack of support of personal needs and maintenance of functioning. Advocacy organizations try these test cases in order to promote and ensure a higher quality of care for nursing home residents.

Another reason that advocacy groups use litigation is to bring public attention to a social problem. Sawin (2005) reports on environmental groups who have brought at least 10 lawsuits against private corporations for failing to address their contribution to global warming from numerous fossil fuel projects financed with taxpayer money. The lawsuits are designed to bring attention to the problem of climate change and to force large polluters to reduce their CO_2 emissions. As with all forms of judicial policy practice, change is slow and incremental, even if the courts rule in favor of our clients. However, it does set precedents for future cases, and should be accompanied by policy practice strategies that focus on parallel reform efforts through legislative and community-based advocacy.

Class Action Lawsuits

Although class action lawsuits are slow, they have the potential to facilitate social and economic changes for large groups of people. Banach, Hamilton, and Perri (2003) conducted a qualitative study on how a class action lawsuit undertaken to require a state to share more of the burden for local education was perceived by the community in which the lawsuit was initiated. The lawsuit contended that the state constitution recognized that the state had a duty to provide an adequate education to every child and to guarantee adequate funding for that education. The Supreme Court decision declared "that a system of financing elementary and secondary education which relied solely on local property taxes was unconstitutional" (p. 83).

Some community members supported the lawsuit, while others who had originally supported the action eventually questioned the results. They were discouraged by negative publicity that the lawsuit incurred and the lack of immediate tax relief. Still others in the community knew little of the lawsuit. Based on the experience of the community, Banach and associates (2003) derive several suggestions for successful class action at the community level.

- Communities need to work together rather than going it alone.
- Communities need information and education regarding the length of time to expect a lawsuit to take.
- Community members need to agree the lawsuit is necessary and to participate in the process.
- Communities must understand that once won, the verdict will have to be implemented and that implementation will need to be monitored.

Policy practitioners can become the bridge between the initiators of the suit and the community. Communication with the community about the problem is needed through strategies such as community awareness campaigns and effective use of the media, as well as effective interpersonal participatory skills, all described in detail in the chapters focusing on strategies.

Class action lawsuits not only rely on a favorable decision by the courts, but people must be aware that there will also have to be subsequent action by the legislators and the executive branch. Basically, this means that if the lawsuit is won, the legislature will have to create policies to accommodate the suit, and they will go through the executive branch's rules and regulations and implementation by agencies. Thus, all of the intervention strategies discussed in Chapter 8, such as testifying before committees, letter writing, and utilizing the media, and Chapter 9, such as commenting on proposed rules and regulations, will need to be utilized to follow through the process to make sure that the lawsuit is carried out the way it was intended.

SUMMARY

This chapter reveals multiple avenues where social work policy practitioners can intervene at the judicial level. Policy practitioners may target specific areas of the court system where change is needed or they can utilize the power of the court to target other systems for change. It is important to notice that in each type of change, organized support is essential, particularly with stakeholders who work with the court system on a regular basis (e.g., lawyers, judges, district attorneys). Social work policy practice is a natural partner in litigation, whether it is individual litigation or class action suits, because of the importance of communication and participation needed in the process when multiple stakeholders are involved. As with other targets of change, the planning process must be utilized with great care to ensure that all potential unintended effects of the goals, objectives, and interventions are considered carefully, that barriers to effective change have been adequately assessed, and that potential support systems are utilized. Finally, remember that judicial policy practice takes time. Review all potential targets before deciding that working through the court system is the best avenue to take. Oftentimes the success or failure of efforts may rely on one judge. And because judgments can be appealed, success at one level may be short lived. Of course, because of the interrelatedness of different sectors of the government, there may well be ways to redress unfavorable outcomes, but time and expense are definitely factors to consider when deciding whether to seek legal remedies to social problems.

TEST YOURSELF

You are a member of the Health Youth Task Force in a medium-sized metropolitan city. The task force works on issues affecting at-risk youth to try to find resources for healthy activities within the city. The task force has recently realized that there is a growing problem of at-risk youth returning to court after being put on probation, either due to new charges or because they have violated probation. The prosecutors and the judge are frustrated. Outpatient treatment has not seemed to work and the population in juvenile detention is growing. The task force also notes that economic opportunities in the city have been declining and the school has recently begun a zero-tolerance policy, which has pushed even more kids into the system.

The task force realizes that to help these kids a more systemic approach to their problems is needed—one that addresses the entire family system as well as the other systems that the families are dealing with. They want to start a community program to help kids and parents work through their own issues and to learn how to work with the other systems to have their needs met. The task force wants to target the court system for referrals, but the judge is skeptical, because none of the other programs have seemed to work in the past. Parenting classes have never been mandatory and therapy almost never includes the parents. The task force is certain that by including the entire family system, working on communication, healthy relationships, building self-esteem, and bringing other systems in the community into the program, they can make a difference.

1. Describe the problem.

2. Analyze the problem and the policy change needed (target the court system). Who are the stakeholders? What will you need to get people on board? What sources of information can you use to help you design your goals and objectives?

3. Design a broad goal.

4. Derive measurable objectives to meet the goal. You can use process objectives (i.e., what needs to be done to get the court system to buy in and to get a good program set up?) and outcome objectives (what it will look like when it is set up and how it will meet the goal).

5. Brainstorm possible strategies and tactics to meet the objectives. These should include ways to get the judge, DA, and probation officers on board, as well as how to get the community/systems to buy into the program.

6. Assess the advantages and disadvantages for each possible strategy.

7. Choose the best tactics with the least obstacles.

8. Provide a rationale for your choices.

9. Provide a plan to evaluate your progress toward your goal.

References

American Bar Association. (2003). Landmark ABA report charts new course for state judicial selection, restoring public trust and confidence in the courts. ABA standing committee on judicial independence. News release retrieved 10/20/06 from www.abanet.org/judind/jeopardy/release.html

Andersen, M., & Collins, P. (2001). *Race, class and gender* (4th ed.). Belmont, CA: Wadsworth/Thomson.

Baig, E. (2005, March 13). Cell phone use booms, despite uneven service. *USA Today*.

Banach, M., Hamilton, D., & Perri, P. (2003). Class action lawsuits. *Journal of Community Practice, 11*, 81–99.

Bednar, S. G. (2003). Elements of satisfying organizational climates in child welfare agencies. *Families in Society, 84*, 7–15.

Berry, J. (1999). *The new liberalism: The rising power of citizen groups.* Washington, DC: Brookings Institute.

Brody, R. (1985). *Legislative process: An action handbook for Ohio's citizen group.* Cleveland, OH: The Federation for Community Planning.

Burkey, S. (1993). *People first: A guide to self-reliant, participatory rural development.* New York: Zed.

Canes-Wrone, B. (2003). Bureaucratic decisions and the composition of the lower courts. *American Journal of Political Science, 47*, 205–214.

Carpenter, S. (1999). Choosing appropriate consensus building techniques and strategies. In L. Susskind, S. McKearnan, & J. Thomas-Larner (Eds.), *The consensus building handbook: A comprehensive guide to reaching agreement* (pp. 61–97). Thousand Oaks, CA: Sage.

Castelloe, P., Watson, T., & White, C. (2002). Participatory change: An integrative approach. *Journal of Community Practice, 10*, 1–32.

Chambers, D., Pearson, J., Lubell, K., Brandon, S., O'Brien, K., & Zinn, J. (2005). The science of public messages for suicide prevention: A workshop summary. *Suicide and Life-Threatening Behavior, 35*, 134–145.

Cragan, J., Wright, D., & Kasch, C. (2004). *Communication in small groups: Theory, process, skills.* Belmont, CA: Wadsworth/Thompson Learning.

Cunningham, C., Woodward, C., Shannon, H., MacIntosh, J., Lendrum, B., Rosenbloom, D., et al. (2002). *Journal of Occupational and Organizational Psychology, 75*, 377–392.

D'Aprix, R., & Gay, C. (2006). Change for the better. *Communication World, 23*, 37–39.

Dewees, S. (1999). The strengths perspective: A first step in empowerment. *The Journal of Baccalaureate Social Work, 4,* 95–108.

Downes, A. (2004). MADD's court monitoring program makes a difference. MADDvocate. Retrieved January 8, 2007, from www.madd.org/madd_programs/10335

Elliott, M. (1999). The role of facilitators, mediators, and other consensus building practitioners. In L. Susskind, S. McKearnan, & J. Thomas-Larner (Eds.), *The consensus building handbook: A comprehensive guide to reaching agreement* (pp. 199–240). Thousand Oaks, CA: Sage.

Engstrom, R., & Kenny, C. (2002). The effects of independent expenditures in Senate elections. *Political Research Quarterly, 55,* 885–905.

Ezell, M. (2001). *Advocacy in the human services.* Belmont, CA: Brooks/Cole.

Federal Election Commission. (2004). 2004 Presidential Popular Vote Summary. Retrieved October 20, 2006, from www.fec.gov/pubrec/fe2004/tables.pdf

Figueira-McDonough, J. (1993). Policy practice: The neglected side of social work intervention. *Journal of Social Work, 38,* 179–188.

Fisher, J. (1999). What will it take to take to transform your organization in the 21st century? *Journal for Quality and Participation, 22*(6), 7–13.

Fisher, R. (1995). Political social work. *Journal of Social Work Education, 31,* 194–203.

Fisher, R. (1996). Neighborhood organizing: The importance of historical context. In W. D. Keating, N. Krumholz, & P. Star (Eds.), *Revitalizing urban neighborhoods* (pp. 39–40). Lawrence: University of Kansas Press.

Foster-Fisherman, P. G., & Keys, C. B. (1997). The person/environment dynamics of employee empowerment: An organizational culture analysis. *American Journal of Community Psychology, 25,* 345–369.

Frans, D. J. (1993). A scale for measuring social worker empowerment. *Research on Social Work Practice, 3,* 312–328.

Furlong, G. (2005). *The conflict resolution toolbox: Models and maps for analyzing, diagnosing, and resolving conflict.* Mississauga, Ontario: Wiley.

Galambos, C., Dulmus, C., & Wodarski, J. (2005). Principles for organizational change in human service agencies. *Journal of Human Behavior in the Social Environment, 11,* 63–78.

Galanes, G., Adams, K., & Brilhart, J. (2004). *Effective group discussion: Theory and practice.* New York: McGraw-Hill.

General Accounting Office. (2002). Strategies for assessing how information dissemination contributes to agency goals. Report to Congressional Committees. GAO 02-023. Washington, DC: United States General Accounting Office.

Gordon, E. B. (1994). Promoting the relevance of policy to practice: Using the ADA to teach social practice. *Journal of Teaching in Social Work, 19,* 165–176.

Gray, V., & Lowery, D. (2001). The institutionalization of state communities of organizer interests. *Political Research Quarterly, 51,* 265–284.

Gutierrez, L., Alvarez, A., Nemon, H., & Lewis, E. (1996). Multicultural community organizing: A strategy for change. *Journal of Social Work, 41,* 501–508.

Gutierrez, L., GlenMaye, L., & Delois, K. (1995). The organizational context of empowerment practice: Implications for social work administration. *Journal of Social Work, 40,* 249–258.

Gutterman, N., & Bargal, D. (1996). Social workers' perception of their power and service outcomes. *Administration in Social Work, 20,* 1–20.

Hardina, D. (2003). Linking citizen participation to empowerment practice: A historical overview. *Journal of Community Practice, 11,* 11–38.

Haynes, K., & Mickelson, J. (2003). *Affecting change: Social workers in the political arena.* Boston: Pearson/Allyn & Bacon.

Hoefer, R. (1999). Social work policy initiatives. *Journal of Community Practice, 6,* 71–87.

Hoefer, R. (2001). Highly effective human service interest groups: Seven key practices. *Journal of Community Practice, 9,* 1–13.

Hoefer, R. (2005). Altering state policy: Interest group effectiveness among state-level advocacy groups. *Social Work, 50,* 219–228.

Hoefer, R. (2006). *Advocacy practice for social justice.* Chicago: Lyceum.

Hojnacki, M., & Kimball, D. (2001). PAC contributions and lobbying contacts in congressional committees. *Political Research Quarterly, 54,* 161–180.

Howell, W. G., & Lewis, D. E. (2002). Agencies by presidential design. *Journal of Politics, 64,* 1095–1114.

Hyde, C. (2003). Multicultural organizational development in non-profit human service agencies: Views from the field. *Journal of Community Practice, 11,* 39–60.

Jansson, B. (2003). *Becoming an effective policy advocate* (4th ed.). Pacific Grove, CA: Brooks/Cole.

Johns, M. (2002). A "one strike" battle planned. Residents journal. Retrieved October 23, 2006, from www.wethepeoplemedia.org/articles/maryjohns/onestrikebattle/

Kaitin, K. (1994). Congressional responses to families in the workplace: The Family and Medical Leave Act of 1987–1988. In F. Jacobs & M. Davies (Eds.), *More than kissing babies? Current child and family policy in the United States* (pp. 91–120). Westport, CT: Auburn House.

Lens, V. (2002). Managed care and the judicial system. *Health and Social Work, 27,* 27–36.

Linhorst, D. (2002). Federalism and social work justice: Implications for social work. *Journal of Social Work, 47,* 201–208.

Maerowitz, M., & Mauet, T. (2003). *Fundamentals of litigation for paralegals.* New York: Aspen.

McInnis-Dittrich, K. (1994). *Integrating social welfare policy and social work practice.* Pacific Grove, CA: Brooks/Cole.

Melber, A. (2006, May 30). Myspace, my politics. *The Nation*, retrieved on July 17, 2006, from www.thenation.com/doc/20060612/melber

Michigan Public Policy Institute. (2001). *Guide to getting good media coverage*. Lansing: Council of Michigan Foundations.

Mizrahi, T., & Rosenthal, B. (2001). Complexities of coalition building: Leaders successes, strategies, struggles, and solutions. *Social Work, 46,* 63–79.

National Association of Social Workers. (1999). Code of Ethics. Retrieved January 2, 2007, from http://www.socialworkers.org/pubs/code/code.asp

National Council for Adoption. (2005). National Council for Adoption Advocates next step in foster care reform. National Council for Adoption Human Services News. Retrieved October 23, 2006, from www.adoptioncouncil.org/documents/Adoption_Advocate_Vol_NO1_06_05.pdf

O'Connor, D. (2002). Toward empowerment: Revisioning family support groups. *Social Work with Groups, 25,* 37–56.

Office of Management and Budget. (2004). Memorandum for the heads of executive departments and agencies. Executive office of the President. Available at www.whitehouse.gov/omb/memoranda/fy2005/m05-04.pdf

Organisation for Economic Co-operation and Development. (2001). *Devolution and globalization: Implications for local decision makers*. Paris: Author.

Petter, J., Byrnes, P., & Choi, D. (2002). Dimensions and patterns in employee empowerment: Assessing what matters to street-level bureaucrats. *Journal of Public Administration and Theory, 12,* 377–400.

Pew Charitable Trust. (2006). Internet activities. Retrieved on July 24, 2006, from www.pewinternet.org/trenda/internet_activities_7.19.06.htm

Pick, M. (1993). *The Sierra Club guide to community organizing: How to save your neighborhood, city, or town*. San Francisco: Sierra Club.

Quinn, M. (2006). Revisiting Anna Moscowitz Kross's critique of New York City's women's court: The continued problem of solving the "problem" of prostitution with specialized criminal courts. *Fordham Urban Law Journal, 33,* 665–726.

Raffa, T. (2000). Advocacy and lobbying without fear: What is allowed within a 501(c)(3) charitable organization. *Nonprofit Quarterly, 7*(2), 1–5.

Richan, W. (1996). *Lobbying for social change*. Binghampton, NY: Haworth Press.

Riley, C., Wersma, J., & Belmarez, D. (2006, June 17). Metro kids behind in home web access: Disparity puts local students at disadvantage, schools fear. *Nashville Tennessean*.

Rocha, C. (2000). Evaluating experiential teaching methods in a policy practice course: The case for service learning to increase political participation. *Journal of Social Work Education, 36*(1), 53–63.

Rocha, C., & Johnson, A. (1997). Teaching family policy through a policy practice framework. *Journal of Social Work Education, 33,* 433–443.

Rose, S. (1999). Social workers as municipal legislators: Potholes, garbage and social activism. *Journal of Community Practice, 6,* 1–14.

Satterfield, B. (2006). What can social networking do for your organization? Retrieved May 5, 2006, from www.techsoup.org/howto/artiles/internet/page4455 .cfm?rss=1

Sawin, J. (2005). Everybody talks about the weather . . . and now they're suing, too. *World Watch, 18,* p. 9.

Schneider, R., & Lester, L. (2001). *A new framework for action: Social work advocacy.* Belmont, CA: Brooks/Cole.

Schwartz, E. (2002). Netactivism 2001: How citizens use the internet. In S. Hick & J. McNutt (Eds.), *Advocacy, activism, and the Internet: Community organization and social policy* (pp. 81–93). Chicago: Lyceum.

Sharwell, G. (1982). How to testify before a legislative committee. In M. Mahaffey & J. Hanks (Eds.), *Practical politics, social work and political responsibility* (pp. 85–98). Silver Spring, MD: NASW.

Shera, W., & Page, J. (1995). Creating more effective human service organizations through strategies of empowerment. *Administration in Social Work, 19,* 1–15.

Steyaert, J. (2002). Inequality and the digital divide: Myths and realities. In S. Hick & J. McNutt (Eds.), *Advocacy, activism, and the Internet: Community organization and social policy* (pp. 199–211). Chicago: Lyceum.

Stoesz, D. (1993). Community with the public. *Social Work, 38,* 367–368.

Stollar, S., Path R., Curtis, M., & Cohen, R. (2006). Collaborative strategic planning as illustration of the principles of systems change. *School of Psychology Review, 35,* 181–197.

Strauss, D. (1999). Designing a consensus building process using a graphic road map. In L. Susskind, S. McKearnan, & J. Thomas-Larner (Eds.), *The consensus building handbook: A comprehensive guide to reaching agreement* (pp. 137–167). Thousand Oaks, CA: Sage.

Studdert, D., & Stevenson, D. (2004). Nursing home litigation and tort reform: A case for exceptionalism. *The Gerontologist, 44,* 588–595.

Tessler, J. (2006, July 7). Senate bill would allow broadband providers to prioritize traffic on their networks. *CQ Congressional Quarterly Weekly,* p. 01878.

Tichenor, D., & Harris, R. (2002/2003). Organized interests and American political development. *Political Science Quarterly, 117,* 587–613.

Ting-Toomey, S., & Oetzel, J. (2001). *Managing intercultural conflict effectively.* Thousand Oaks, CA: Sage.

Turner, R. (2002). Public policy technology and the non-profit sector: Notes from the field. In S. Hick & J. McNutt (Eds.), *Advocacy, activism, and the Internet: Community organization and social policy* (pp. 43–57). Chicago: Lyceum.

Tyuse, S., & Linhorst, D. (2005). Drug courts and mental health courts: Implications for social work. *Health and Social Work, 30,* (3), 1–10.

Uehara, E., Sohng, S., Bending, R., Seyfried, S., Richey, C., Morelli, P., et al. (1996). Toward a values-based approach to multicultural social work research. *Journal of Social Work, 41,* 613–623.

U.S. Census Bureau. (2004). U.S. cell phone use up more than 300 percent, Statistical Abstract reports. News Release CB04-236. Retrieved July 20, 2006, from www .census.gov/press-release/archives/miscellaneous

U.S. Congress. Senate. *The Family Medical Leave Act.* (1993). 29 U.S.C. 2654, 60 FR 2237.

Weil, M., & Gamble, D. (1995). Community practice models. In Richard Edwards (Ed.), *Encyclopedia of social work, 19th edition* (pp. 577–593). Washington, DC: NASW.

Wilson, R. (2005, Feb. 3). SAHA wrongly cited feds in eviction: Agency to weigh new drug policy in wake of zero-tolerance stance. *San Antonio Express News,* p. 3b.

Wyers, N. L. (1991). Policy practice in social work: Models and issues. *Journal of Social Work Education, 27,* 241–250.

Yackee, S. (2005). Sweet-talking the fourth branch: The influence of interest group comments on federal agency rulemaking. *Journal of Public Administration Research and Theory, 16,* 103–124.

Yorke, Carl. (2003). *The candidate's handbook for winning state and local elections.* Palo Alto, CA: Political Net Press.

Zimmerman, M., & Rappaport, J. (1988). Citizen participation, perceived control, and psychological empowerment. *American Journal of Community Psychology, 16*(5), 725–750.

Index